Poet, thinker, writer and metaphysical philosopher, Neil David Chan is the author of his new book: *A Higher Conversation – Another Way to Be Human.* Being a well-traveled, cosmopolitan writer, Neil has extensively absorbed the languages, backgrounds, religions, and cultures of our uniquely beautiful planet. *A Higher Conversation* is the culmination of collective wisdom, discovery, and inspiration derived from his many years of writing, travel, and exploration.

Neil strongly believes in how humans are constructed as a three aspect being body, mind and soul. He believes that our soul has and is, a misunderstood metaphysical entity. Using his deep belief and understanding, he was able to connect with his soul to begin a higher conversation. Neil uses his soul as his compass all the time to navigate his way through life. Through his book, he hopes to illuminate this same compass for others so that they can discover their untapped potential and practice another way to be human.

His second book is on its way. He is passionate about making a difference in the world to help others find their compass. Neil lives ánd writes from Toronto, Canada, the true North, with his wife. They have two children. He spends his summer hiking and camping with his wife and their friends. Neil loves watching basketball, his favorite team: NBA champions – Toronto Raptors. He also mixes a mean cocktail.

To my wonderful wife, Heera, and my two lovely children, Nyshka and Varun, all of whom have gifted me far more than I have.

Neil David Chan

A HIGHER CONVERSATION

Another Way to Be Human

AUSTIN MACAULEY PUBLISHERS™

LONDON • CAMBRIDGE • NEW YORK • SHARJAH

Ordering Information:
Quantity sales: special discounts are available on quantity purchases by corporations, associations, and others. For details, contact the publisher at the address below.

Publisher's Cataloging-in-Publication data
Chan, Neil David
A Higher Conversation

ISBN 9781645363828 (Paperback)
ISBN 9781645363811 (Hardback)
ISBN 9781645363842 (ePub e-book)

Library of Congress Control Number: 2020908950

www.austinmacauley.com/us

First Published (2020)
Austin Macauley Publishers LLC
40 Wall Street, 28th Floor
New York, NY 10005
USA

mail-usa@austinmacauley.com
+1 (646) 5125767

I would want to start by thanking the most wonderful people in my world – you the readers. You make all of this hard work worth it. Thank you for reading my book and for telling people about them. I also want to thank the booksellers who ignite passion for reading but also encourage and empower many readers. Thank you for bringing my book and the readers together. I also want to say a big thank you to Austin Macauley Publishers for publishing my book, *A Higher Conversation* and to everyone in their team who worked with me to proofread, publish and market. Without their help and support, this book would never see the daylight, it is seeing today. So thank you from the bottom of my heart. I also want to give a big shout out to the team from Toronto Web Design for helping me early on to design and decorate my webpage and website with book cover images, blurbs and blogs and for Andrei's constant support and guidance. Finally, I get to thank my wonderful family for supporting me, encouraging me, motivating me before, during and after my writing. They were absolutely fantastic, as always. I also want to acknowledge that I had wonderful parents, a loving family, and several spiritual teachers, who along the way shaped my thinking. I also acknowledge my faith and my soul, without which this book would not have been possible.

The True Essence
of a Human Being

Relativity is an extremely critical component of human relationships and physical life. It is the essential smart core. All human relationships also carry these very same principles of special and general relativity as discovered by Einstein.

We have all grown up the Euclidean way, named after the Alexandrian Greek mathematician Euclid. That is the only way we know. Our minds are conditioned, and hence we are unable to see things in any other way. This conditioning, over the years, has hardened, disabling us from seeing anything in a new light or through a new filter.

Biology and living must not be combined. While biology is a study of all beautiful living things, life is about celebrating the beauty of life. While biology is a study of existing life forms, life is about existing in a happy, peaceful, and loving way.

Author's Note

Planet Earth is the third planet from our Sun. Earth is about 5 billion years or more old. For life to start planetary atmosphere needs to evolve to allow living conditions. We have gone through three makeovers. As per scientists and studies conducted, our first atmosphere was Helium and Hydrogen. Due to extreme heat, this did not last. Constant volcanic eruptions brought in steam and carbon dioxide. Over billions of years water from the steam condensed to form oceans that today cover most of Earth. Then came the bacteria releasing oxygen and nitrogen. The amount of nitrogen and oxygen expanded and grew to what we have today. Life forms in Earth need oxygen and nitrogen to survive. Nitrogen and Oxygen grew larger and larger, allowing life forms to evolve as per scientific studies conducted by Eco- scientists. Ice appeared 2 billion years ago, and for the last seven hundred thousand years, glacial ice began to expand and contract. About 70,000 years ago, ice started to melt, and around 10,000 years ago it fully melted, leaving large blocks around the Artic and Antarctica. Life started to evolve on the planet. Animals, plants, and trees began to appear, and finally human beings. We evolved while our planet cooled and evolved to make way for us, to make it our habitat. This is planetary and human evolution collaborating with each other to co-exist and form a relationship to self-support each other. It was a great collaboration and a relationship, the planet supporting life forms on it and the life forms respecting the planet and its atmosphere. This story, unfortunately, did not last long.

Human beings no longer respect the planet and its atmosphere like they did in the past. This relationship is now fully broken. Our relationship with our body, mind, and soul is also broken. Our relationships with humanity as a whole, with our community, with our close family and with our neighbors are also broken in many ways. We no longer understand how to create, sustain, and grow relationships. This is where my higher conversation begins, from all of these broken relationships.

Like everyone, I had a lot of questions—what if, why not, and so on. I was not able to get any clear answers, so I kept talking to myself and one day, a new feeling came along, followed by a thought. So I paused and told myself, someone is giving you answers to the questions that you are asking. I did not know the answer and now I do. So I wondered who this can be. And I got an answer to that too. Suddenly, I knew I had a new friend, a new connection. So I asked all of my questions with a pure desire to know. This started a new conversation with a new friend and today, this friend is my BFF. At this very moment, I was introduced to my soul. Once this experience took place, I became aware that I have three aspects—my body, my mind, and my soul. I accepted this and began to engage all three aspects to create my experiences. It still is a work in progress, but I am aware and awake. While my thoughts, words, and deeds are not fully synchronized with my body, mind, and soul, I am trying hard to make it so. My struggle is getting better, my filter is reducing, and my alignment is working itself slowly to make the fusion, the unity, and the merge permanent. My physicality is overemphasized and my metaphysicality is underemphasized. I am working to balance this and this is going to be a process, a slow one but a sure one.

Relativity and physicality are two very important aspects of our life on earth. Breaking relationships in both areas is neither evolution nor elevation of our species. We cannot grow and develop until we mend this. So I started my quest, a search to discover my soul. This ended up in a beautiful relationship. Over many years, I have had many conversations with my soul. Of course, the language of the soul is by feelings only; however, these feelings can become thoughts that can be scribed and transcribed. I assembled these thoughts and transcribed them into words. We can all do this. The degree of difficulty slowly becomes easier over time, if you are laser-focused. We are all used to talking to a person, face to face.

This is the physicality of our human existence so far. So it is very hard to listen to your feelings and transcribe it as words. Our bodies and minds are familiar to us. We understand this as the body being physical and the mind being nonphysical and the generator of thoughts. Using our thoughts, we get the body to do things we want to do. While this is second nature to us, the soul is still alien for nearly everyone, simply because we do not understand nor accept. We never practice engaging our soul, which is a metaphysical aspect of us. Although the mind is also a metaphysical aspect, we have grown up using our minds. This makes our mind familiar. We have never engaged our soul, so this is unfamiliar and we are not comfortable with unfamiliarity, another issue of too much physicality. We need to let our minds forget the past and use it to link to new feelings our soul puts out. Over time, our mind starts to delete our past ways of doing things and starts a new way to do things. This is the change that I am writing about.

We have all grown up the Euclidean way, named after the Alexandrian Greek mathematician Euclid. That's the only way we know. Our minds are conditioned, and hence we are unable to see things in any other way. This conditioning, over the years, has hardened, disabling us from seeing anything in a new light or through a new filter. A conversation with our soul can help remove this conditioning, reduce our filter, and open a wormhole into new dimensions. We are all on the cusp of a new beginning of our final journey, our last mile home. All we need to do is dial up 1-800-Soul and start noticing the feelings. You will be amazed at where this will take you. Like Alice in Wonderland, you will go to places you never knew existed, ideas you never knew, and begin a new understanding of another way to be human.

It's hard to talk to a metaphysical aspect of yourself. It is very unsettling, and most times, it sounds unreal. However, when you come into this with a firm belief that you need to make friends with your soul, it helps a lot. When I became aware that what I knew was not helping me, I wanted to wipe clean all of my past understanding and begin a new understanding. This is how my conversation started and then rolled into new places. It's not easy; the daily grind of life gets into you and the daily distraction takes you away. Body fat, ego from your mind, financial debt, or excessive wealth keeps many of you distracted from focusing on your soul. This is natural. Allow it to happen, but come back to the road after you have wandered off-road, and continue your journey. It has been a very long one for me. At all times, it feels like you are talking and getting no response. This is true because you are expecting a response in words you can hear. Drop this expectation and look forward to getting a feeling as your response. Words are confusing; feelings are pure. Embrace this slowly and firmly.

As humans, we communicate best face-to-face. This has been so since we existed on earth. In recent years, we have been increasingly exposed to electronic mail, text and electronic messaging, avoiding face-to-face conversations. A vast majority of us are still not willing and ready for a faceless conversation. This makes it hard for us to understand communicating with our soul. There is a high degree of difficulty for our species to understand metaphysical aspects of life. I can totally understand how far away this sounds from a face-to-face conversation. For many, this has been science fiction. Moving from fiction to fact is very challenging. But I tell you, we need to do it, for that's the only way forward for all of us.

And we are not alone; we have help waiting by. Before we accept or call for help, we need to get our home straightened out, and this starts with a conversation with our soul. Only after we have made this first contact with our soul will any help become meaningful. Once our body-mind-soul combination is humming along, then any external help will act as a springboard for us to quantum jump into a higher plane. So I urge all of you to start a conversation. Shed off your conflict-versus-commerce thought pattern. Either we are fighting—conflicting—or engaging in business deals—commerce—or maybe doing a bit of both. Can you see the stereotypical pattern? Starting your conversation with your soul needs no pre-condition and no special skill sets. Just quiet your external and take notice of your internal.

All life forms ingest, metabolize and excrete. This is the core function of our physicality at a basic level. For all transient beings, this is the common denominator. Commerce has blown up the "ingest" part of our prime function. Commerce has also led us to conflict. We are so occupied and preoccupied with ingesting that we have over-loaded our metabolic and excretion systems and brought about disease and suffering. When you compare ingest, metabolize, and excrete with body, mind, and soul, ingest is akin to your body, excrete is akin to your mind and metabolize is akin to your soul. We are ingesting and excreting. The metabolize function has diminished in many people and so, we have developed many forms of diseases. If we can pump up the metabolic ability, many of our body problems will be over. Similarly, if we can engage our soul, many of our human problems will also be over. Given this current over-loaded ingest situation, what chance do we have to move to metaphysical issues? Obsession with our body and with our mind supporting this obsession is isolating you from your soul. This alone calls for starting your conversation with your soul.

I was inspired and encouraged to get in touch with my soul and start a conversation. Armed with this self-confidence, I started a conversation with my soul, and this conversation is what I scribed and transcribed. What followed was an amazing conversation, the depth of which is beyond the world I live in. However, it also helped me to widen my thinking horizon to bring in something new, made alive by the experience of a soulful conversation. Experiencing is everything. We have been told that the best way to understand is to tell it to another. This is what I have done in expressing my experience; this is me telling all of you.

I, as a physical being, was talking to my metaphysical being. I can understand that this can be a non-starter for many of you. A conversation, as we understand it, has always been between two human beings. We talk to God through prayer; this is the normal way of life. We all know this. Because God does not talk back in a human way, we do not get to know the response to our prayers, and so it remains a one-way conversation. When you start to accept that our soul is a miniaturized version of God fully dedicated to you—as a resource to help you as you walk through life—then talking to your soul becomes easy. The saying in our ancient books *"Fear not, I go ahead of you always, follow me, I will give you rest"* now becomes very clear. Your God as your soul is with you and in a way ahead of you: just follow. And follow means listen to the feelings your soul puts out to you and trust the feeling.

It may sound strange that I was able to do this. If you really and truly believe that we are a three-part being, then starting the quest and finding the way to engage with your soul becomes easy. One needs to quiet the external to hear the internal. I did this, tuned in and found the most interesting conversation I never knew was possible. Our soul talks to us all of the time, and this can be picked up as thoughts like a phone receiving a pulse signal and converting the pulse into words you can hear. Similarly, you can convert your feelings into thoughts and then into words, just like the phone does. What a phone does physically, you can do metaphysically. Simple as that.

I struggled to get a grasp, and then slowly, it began to get better. My filter over time reduced, allowing me to get the true message. I was able to feel what my soul was expressing. It takes a long time initially to get it correct; your mind is very clever in superimposing its private agenda and distorting the signal, the message, and the meaning. It became simple for me to understand the clutter over time.

Our mind is always feeding our body or ego desires— nothing else. So the clarity to filter out what the mind is trying to impose on you and what the soul is trying to say gets easier with time. At this point, our soul's message becomes crystal clear. The soul's message will never be about your body or about your ego, so it's easy to segregate what comes from your inside. Although I still struggle with it, over time this has become easier. The struggle is a good thing. It tells you that you are overcoming built-up conditioning, opening up to new thoughts, and reducing the need for your filter in order to understand.

Everything points to the issue of neglecting your soul, building up your body desires, and upsizing your ego. The conversation with your soul can help turn this imbalance to balance. I urge you—I encourage you to make that leap from your body and mind only, to include your soul and see what lies ahead. Discover it for the sake of discovery, for the sake of adventure. It can't hurt you, it may save you, and you have nothing to lose. The experience is awesome. I am awake now and hope you awaken too. Please hurry up—we have miles to go and places to see. I can't go alone. We all have to go, so if you are not ready, we are all not ready. The journey must be collective; only then can we all evolve. Evolution will not allow the pursuit of individual gain and profit on a longer time frame, but it will help if collective gain and profit begin to take shape. Our history has shown this to be true; we have not yet learned and not yet put this into a practiced way of life.

The conversations in my book were transcribed using the regular font for the author and italic font for comments made by my soul for readers to understand the two sources distinctly and differently. I asked my questions and got my answers. You too can ask your own questions and get your own answers. Everyone can and everyone must. Our ancient books have told us *"Ask and Ye Shall get."* So, go ahead and ask anything you want and get your own answers, as I have. Trust me, it's easy; just believe in it and allow it to happen, and it will. I understand every person will surely have different questions, different themes of concern. You will find that each soul will answer specifically to whatever questions you ask but the fundamental truths about universality—about love, joy and peace, and about the three aspects of our being—will always be reinforced no matter what the questions are. Your questions asked and answers given will remove all of your doubts on this.

Your first step is to accept who you are; denying who you really are will not help. Once you have accepted this, also accept that we are composed of three unique aspects— body-mind-soul. These are our buildup tools in life. Don't allow any dogmas, religious or personal, to affect your thinking this way. This is your reality. Only if you accept this can we all move forward. Each aspect has a part and each aspect has a role to play. The body is physical, the mind and the soul are metaphysical. Using all three aspects, we can generate our own experiences, but every time we use only one or two aspects, then our experience changes. The first step is to get to know your soul and make that first introduction, reach out and say hello and let the conversation begin. All of what I have written is an exchange that took place between me, in my body and mind format and my soul. All of what transpired, I have honestly and thoughtfully delivered as a book. I am sharing my process with all of you, in the hope you can create your own processes, and I wish that you do. In that spirit, I invite you to read on.

Introduction

Chapter 1
The Flow

We are a being at our core, a human being composed of three aspects—body, mind, and soul. These three aspects are given to us at birth. These are our build-up tools to grow and evolve. All of us have this. We just don't understand this as a global understanding. While our body and our mind are known to us, our soul is unknown. All religious teachings do not speak about this, but some of our ancient books carry multiple references to our soul. Passages in my book tell you about these references. It's not only me saying this; our ancient books also speak about this. This is a part of you from birth till death and is here to help you.

Your first step is to accept who you are; denying who you really are will not help. Once you have accepted this, also consider that we are composed of three unique aspects—body, mind, and soul. Don't allow any dogmas—religious or personal—affect your thinking. This is your reality. Should you choose to accept this, we can move forward. Each aspect helps you and each aspect has a role to play. Together, they help create the perfect experience for you. The body is physical, the mind and the soul are metaphysical. Using all three aspects, we can generate our own experiences but every time we use only one or two aspects, our experience stays limited.

Look at it like a video game you play. Using all the tools you have collected and the points you have earned, you can play the game to reach the next level and to the final level. Use less tools and you lose lives and levels. Just like this, not using our three aspects, we create experiences that are not in our highest advantage and in our greatest benefit. Bring your soul to the team and see how your game changes and see how you experience things differently, vastly different from what you experience today. And the first step is to get to know your soul and make that first introduction, reach out and say hello and let the conversation begin. Very soon, your soul will become your BFF.

Merriam Webster's dictionary explains conversation as an oral exchange of sentiments, observations, opinions, or ideas. Wikipedia calls conversation interactive communication between two or more people. This book is a conversation I had with my third aspect, my soul. It is an exchange of ideas, observations, and opinions about life. It starts with the opening concept of separation and follows a path on basic human issues that govern our modern society. This is the human **me**, talking to my soul **me**, trying to talk about issues I believe in and asking my soul for guidance and clarification, in order to better understand and look at it differently and find another way to be human.

As I start my conversation with my soul, I speak my mind and my soul responds. All of this is documented in this book. The response was not quick—it took time, several years. I raised my point and the response came in ways I did

21

not understand. Over time, I began to feel the feelings that came across as it converted itself as thoughts. All of this took a lot of time. It was slow but steady, and then, over time, it became easy to interpret the thoughts and scribe.

Albert Einstein's theory of relativity touched and improved upon the science of elementary particles and their fundamental interactions and transformed theoretical physics and astronomy during the 20th century, giving rise to general and special relativity. Relativity is a very critical component of human relationships and physical life. It's the essential smart core. All human relationships also carry these very same principles of special and general relativity as discovered by Einstein. The order of discovery should have been the other way around. From the understanding of human relativity, the relativity among other particles in the universe should have followed. We got the order wrong again. This only shows that while we search for the secrets of the universe, the secrets of human life in our earth continue to stay hidden.

All of humanity is equal in every way in the eyes of our creator. But in the eyes of the people who live here on earth, separation by segregation is given a rank order: wealth, good looking and slim, white skin, position, power and so on at the top, and so many other aspects at the very bottom. And with this order, everything else follows—a whole lot of separation ideology that arranges and places people in different life shelves of importance, with everyone trying to jump shelves to reach the top. While at birth, conditions cannot be changed, material acquisitions can be gained along the way to compensate for lack of top-shelf characteristics. The things that people try to acquire to compensate for lack of top-shelf attributes are several, like education, money, house, car, family, and so on. This list changes all the time; new ones are added, old ones deleted. Items of separation keep on increasing, widening the gap between the haves and the have-nots.

Yes, this is a correct understanding. You are focusing on at-birth conditions and giving them a meaning, whereas you should be focusing on using the differences of at-birth conditions to form a universal team. To speak in the language you understand, in an ice hockey team or in a basketball team, or in a football team, are all people the same? No, different people come together to play a game, excel at it and win. Isn't that what you call team spirit? What happened to this understanding in forming a global team to live life? Why is it that something that works and wins is never used to form a global community team? Now you see how separation and segregation are illogical, because, at the global level, no one wants to win. There are no prizes to give away for a global community team.

Yes, conditions at birth have caused many problems and are also a leading cause of separation. We have so much information, too much of it—even a ten-year-old knows a lot of stuff. All of this information is of no use when the basic core of human life is built on differentiating aspects. I am better than you, I was born different than you, I have better things than you and I will be a better person than you. I hear this all the time. I have not to this day heard someone say, I have a bigger liver than yours or a larger lung than yours. Why not? Because we are all born with the same size lungs and liver. It's a one-size-fits-all creation. So where does this "greater than you" come from?

It comes from modified thought, passed down by generations that you need to be better by portraying yourself as better than others are. Even though all of others have the same sized body parts as brain, heart, lungs, liver and so on, somehow, you need to highlight your acquired possession differences and stay silent on the common human parts. In short, you need to create what the creator didn't create to make you happier than everyone else. Separation at its purest form. Biology and living must not be combined. While biology is a study of all beautiful living things, life is about celebrating the beauty of life. While biology is a study of existing life forms, life is about existing in a happy, peaceful, and loving way. You classified what was created the way your librarian classifies books.

My conversation with you is an attempt to knock at this basic issue and bring in a new understanding of creation and classification. Why were all life forms created? Not for classification and segregation for sure, this much I know.

Life, as you know, is an expression in physicality to experience in physical form what a non-physical form cannot. Individual life forms were created to support all life forms to live in harmony, peace, and joy, loving each other in every way that creates a network of a self-supporting library of life-supporting resources, a vast chain of interdependent life forms, each protecting the other in circular logic. Any network is a sum total of all its smaller parts. Individual parts of the network support the whole of the network; they do not glorify each part. The desire and intent are not to break the chain, but to grow in individual size for the sole purpose of growing the network. The whole of it is the higher ground; each of it is the plain ground. The high ground exists only because of the plain ground. The elevation is from a plain ground; without the plain ground, there is no elevation.

So we assumed the role of a librarian, labeling, categorizing, and placing life forms and people on different shelves. This works well for books and inanimate objects, that don't need any resources to grow. Why did we do this with life?

Life is never inanimate; it is animate, full of energy, interdependent on other life forms for food, growth, and survival. When these things become a shared network of resources meant for all to share and for all to grow, there can only be one shelf—no top shelf and no bottom shelf. Living beings cannot be placed on a hierarchical ladder. This makes people in the lower rung of the ladder try and climb up the ladder, unmindful of the ways used to trample, destroy, choke, abuse, and kill people on the way and on the climb up. Take away the ladder and take away the shelves, people will start moving sideways. This is way better because there is plenty of space on a plain path compared to a narrow ladder. Life was never meant to be labeled, classified, segregated, or divided into smaller portions. It was always meant to be clarified as one large community, living in different places, protected against the sun and the sunlight for sustained reproduction.

Separation

Chapter 2
The Fracturing of the Three
Aspects of Our Being

This is a subject matter that I have always held dear and strong. So my conversation was very intense. Today, separation has acquired a life and an ideology of its own— The Separation Ideology. We are organic sentient beings at the core. We are human beings in three aspects or in three parts, as we now know. This is important to remember. This is important too, as we continue with this conversation. Body, mind, and soul are the three aspects of our human existence.

Yes, this is true; each of your aspects comes with an inbuilt desire and stays independent until you decide to merge them together to form one unified working aspect. This is possible when you understand your three aspects better. Don't they say to know is the first step, to understand the next step and to accept, the final step? I see that you are using the word aspect to differentiate from body parts, so let's stay with it. The mind and the soul are not visible to a human eye. They are there; trust it and believe it. The mind is like a computer in a metaphysical form; the soul is an energy source, also in a metaphysical form. The body is visible and in a physical form. A physical form with two metaphysical aspects—that is who you truly are in your human form. In reality, you are a metaphysical being in a physical form. Somehow, you consider yourself the other way around—a body with a soul. In reality, you are a spirit with a body. A true understanding of this will set you free from your current mental construction.

We have fractured these three aspects. It's up to us to decide how we use the three gifts we were given or how we choose not to use them. All of us typically use the body-mind combination to grow. Although all of us have free will to choose the combination we prefer, the body-mind combination is our current widely-used format.

This has not yet produced the results you need and seek. While you have no obligation to do anything, doing nothing does not serve your purpose to grow. That's the beauty of your creation—no obligation, no compulsion to do anything particular. It's totally up to you as individual beings to choose your path, the one you want to take. The tools and the resources for growth have been placed at your disposal from birth. It's your choice to use, abuse, or avoid; you have free will, and this is your creator's way to show love for all life. Without free will, there is no choice; without choice, there is no free will; without free will, there is no love. All three are bound to each other in circular logic. Another set of tools that are at your disposal are awareness and consciousness. They are not the same although many of you think they are. They are two different tools. Awareness happens when you use all three aspects to decide and express who you really are. When you continue doing this repeatedly, making it a habit, you start to raise your consciousness. Your energy starts to vibrate more strongly around you. At this stage, you can consider this as enlightenment. You can all reach this point. It's not a point reserved for a few; it's meant for all of you. You could say awareness is an action you take consciously to raise your level of consciousness.

This means that not just a chosen few are earmarked for enlightenment. All of us have an equal opportunity to attain this level of understanding. All we need is to start moving towards this point, recognize our three aspects and start linking, syncing, and using them. Use all three aspects to make a move in life, make a decision, start a thought process, or say something to another. For every thought we think, for every word we speak, for every deed we do, allow the three aspects to collaborate and come to a joint agreement. This will avoid body-focused decisions or mind-only thoughts or acts done using the body-mind combination. This is what I am understanding.

Yes, this is correct. Doing this will produce the result that is useful to you in your development as you become a highly-evolved being. These three words are very powerful: **high** *comes from your thinking,* **evolved** *comes from the habit of using all three aspects—the body, the mind, and the soul—and in doing so, the* **being** *now becomes complete, hence the expression—***highly evolved being.**

That was easy to understand. We should all aim to become highly-evolved beings as we live our lives on earth. And for this to happen, all of us need to use all the three aspects in balance and harmony. The more the connection, the more the unity, the greater is the consciousness. I get it now.

You are given options all the time; you just don't see it this way. All the roads open up right in front of you and for your own different reasons; you simply ignore this. You are not fully awake; you're just starting to awaken after billions of years. A call to awaken was made long ago. Most of you are not listening. All of you are busy trying to make a profitable life. There is too much external information you are chasing. You can never internalize all of this. All that you need is available to you at the soul level; just remember and re-member with your soul.

When we use external information as our source to create options, we are simply merging into the opinion expressed by others, forgetting our ancient library—the library of our soul. What use is this to us? No wonder the media and all written material do their best to influence us. We are swayed easily, we are influenced too quickly, only because we have not engaged our soul in interacting with external information. This leaves us without soul care, similar to no parental care for a child.

Working from your mind which has nothing but your past experiences, labeled and categorized, you are repeating and repeating everything you have done in the past under new circumstances. Everything that happens is here and now. At any time, there is only the present moment. Look at your soul to seek wisdom from its ancient library available to you for guidance, with no need for a library card or a membership. You are a lifelong member of this library. How many of you use this seriously? This is your soul available to guide your living; use it well and use it all the time. This is the seat of consciousness, where your true being resides, silently waiting for you to come knocking on its doors. The mind is not a place of wisdom, not your go-to; it's merely a processing tool. But what are you processing? Desires of the body supported by the mind. All of humanity from inception has been doing the mind-body routine. Where has this taken you? Look at the world you now live in. The answer is clear, visible, and loud. You are not evolving. You are reproducing all right, too fast I would say, and this is only just one part of evolution, just the starting point. You have taken several billion years to evolve, and yet, you are still not far from the starting point. You need to step it up, as you would say in your language, take it several notches higher.

How can we do this when we only know our body and mind? As I understand our mind, the second metaphysical aspect is like an advanced processor that creates our thoughts based on what we want it to be. Like Aladdin's lamp, it fulfills the body desires that we call for with a slight difference—it does not create matter or material things. It brings to us an experience as our reality, where we can fulfill all of our wants.

Yes, if that's what you want, you will get the experience of wanting. Aladdin's lamp was a story only to highlight an ancient truth, that all of mankind's wants only matter and material, gold and more gold, a palace and more palaces, and so on. Matter and material are never a true inspiration for greatness; the pursuit of this is only playing to your deep body desire to acquire things other than what you really need. The mind is built to be loyal to the body because the body is vulnerable. It's the weakest of the three aspects and therefore needs protection. It's a babysitter for the body. Since the body is a physical form, it is easily subject to damage. The mind gives it protection by providing a shield. So remember this, the mind works to protect your body; it should not be confused as the seat of higher learning or the originator of higher thoughts. Your mind is simply a powerful processor, pre-programmed to serve and protect your body, totally loyal and biased to your body. While this is important for your survival, it is not inclusive because it is not meant to be. That part and role belongs to your soul, your third aspect. That is the soul's job description, as you would say in your world. This mind-body combination served you well during your survival times when your ancestors lived in hostile environments and conditions. It is no longer relevant today; survival as an instinct needs to become extinct. You no longer need this instinct. Survival is not an issue today. Growth and development of the human being is the real need today. You need to develop beyond muscle and mass. When you are threatened, fear and anger increase your reflexes and, to some degree, your strength. This was useful during the times of your ancestors to run from the saber-toothed tiger and hunt for meat. It no longer serves your purpose today.

I am now beginning to understand my mind and its loyalty to my body. All this time, I thought this was where my higher side was coming from. This was an error in my understanding, but then, I never knew anything about my soul. Understanding my three aspects opened my filter and here I am talking to you, my soul. So what is our body?

The body—your third aspect—is what you all identify yourselves with, simply because you can see, feel and touch. Sensory perception is still a strong human way of life. This is your physical stage of evolution. It's time to get past this and move on to your next level. You are unable to see the mind and the soul so, therefore, you do not understand what they are. They are metaphysical aspects, not visible; one needs feelings to feel these two aspects. You were told that your body actually is just a shell you were given as the natural habitat of the mind and the soul. This allows the body to experience the beauty of life and express it, having experienced it. It serves a purpose but not the only purpose; it is a one-third member, not the full member. The other two members being the mind and the soul. Today, you live, making the body the only member you know. It's time to get to know your neighbors, it's time to communalize all three members, and it's time to form a community of your body, mind, and soul. When you start to form this internal community, you will learn to make other external human communities. Inclusion starts here. This is your learning opportunity; here is your classroom and your teacher.

Embrace this as your lesson, and everything else will become easier to understand. To illustrate this, let's say you love your coffee or your tea. Without a cup, holder, or container, you can never experience the taste of coffee or tea, because you can't drink it. The cup is akin to your body and the coffee is akin to your soul. Without the body, the soul is unable to experience. Now the concept of the soul with the body should become clearer to you.

We are trying to understand all of this; it's so new to us. No one told us all these things until we were told. So the body was designed to provide an experience to our soul and act as a shell for the soul to reside in. And, being a body, it fulfills physical functions like breathing, eating, and excreting. As long as it lives, it creates an opportunity for the soul to experience. And when the body and the mind understand this, the body will experience the joy the soul will experience. This is collective joy.

Yes, this is a correct understanding. When you want only the body to experience, you get a very low level of experience. Bring the mind and the soul to the party and your experience will rise exponentially. At the functional core of your human being, you ingest, you metabolize, and you excrete. Only a body can do this and your body is designed to do all these three things with precision and clockwork. If and when these three functions do not work properly, that's when you should realize something is wrong fundamentally with your body.

So this is the physicality of our living experience. I think we have given this too much importance and made it our only way of life. As I understand, our body is like the display screen of a computer. How we engage our mind and our soul is displayed on our body. It is a reflection of the mind-soul usage. That's why we see human bodies in different shapes and forms, in different health and disease levels. The body displays how your inner contents are working or, more importantly, how you have engaged your mind and soul or how you have not engaged them. All of us engage this combination in some way or another. It's the level of usage and the true understanding of the usage that gets displayed in your body. The computer displays whatever commands are used inside an application. So too, our body shows how well or how much we have used the mind-soul combination. Hence, there is a saying that goes, "Don't live in your body." Right!

Yes, so true. The body-mind dual combo is simply one way to live, not the best way. Remember the mind is protecting your body and will always do so, as long as you live. This code cannot be changed. However, the soul does not need any protection. It cannot be damaged nor its energy reduced. It is immortal in its basic design, stays with you as long as you need it and goes away when it's time to go. Your mind helps the body by using its memory of how you executed a similar task in the past and then adjusts to suit the current task. It's your AI—artificial intelligence. Your real intelligence is with the soul. Always remember your mind is pre-wired to serve your body needs only. Can you expect more from your mind? You can, but in reality, no, every move your mind makes is heavily biased to serve your body from a survival point of view, anticipating famine or danger to your body and compensating by additional glandular and cellular internal secretions. Always remember, evolution favors the survival of the species; the mind favors the survival of your body. Evolution is a higher intelligence; your mind has only your life's experiences to execute. One can say this is your mind's prime directive, to serve and protect your body. While evolution is ancient wisdom, your mind is built on acquired wisdom from you. There is a huge quantum difference between the two. Depending on your mind is like repeating your ways of life executed until now; hence, it is very limited and not probably the most reliable resource. This is where the balance comes in—when you merge all three aspects, each working to its best ability for the body as a shell to move through life. The mind is a powerful processor designed to help your body, and the soul is your guide to your mind and body. It can lead you to higher aspects and prospects of life that your body and your mind are not yet aware of. Your soul stays silent most of the time unless you call for it. It is like an on-call service, activated when called. Of all the options that come to you, "What will you choose now?" is a question that has presented itself to all of you since life evolved. Ask your soul and then wait for the answer to come to you.

So today we have fractured our three aspects. We use our body primarily to create body desires and body experiences and our mind happily supports this. The mind protects the body and gives our body what it wants. We have forgotten our soul. Isn't this separation and fracture?

Although you can try to separate, the basic design is too strong to stay separated; someday, you will merge, maybe not in your current lifetime, but over many lifetimes or maybe in this lifetime! Separation ends up creating a dissonance, a distortion in your bio-sphere. The three aspects stay separate. This causes a lot of grief and your body is always the only recipient of this grief because only the body has a form. The impact affects a form only. The distortion and the dissonance do not affect your mind or your soul. All physical forms are subject to impact. In staying separate, you bring harm to your body unconsciously. Disease, depression, damage, and death are some of the consequences of this separation ideology. Why do you choose for these to happen when there is an easy way out? Simply use all three aspects to live and say goodbye to disease, depression, and damage. Isn't this simple and easy to do?

It sounds simple but is so hard to do. I guess, over millions of years, using our body and mind as our only known resources, the soul today remains as our unknown resource. The idea and the knowledge that we are a three-aspect being is now slowly coming into our focus. We were shown this aspect we never knew. We have always lived separately from nature and from all of the resources of nature, just like the way we stay separate from our soul and its vast resources. We continue this behavior with human life too. We stay separated from all of humanity, and we find some convenient reason to justify this. The separation that started with color spread to our thoughts and belief systems. Over the years, today it has become the root cause for all our misery. We do not accept our three aspects. We favor only our body and this has created an inbuilt mechanism to embrace separation. As this ideology gained traction, separation became a universal application across all things and thoughts.

Remember, your mind is very powerful; it gives you what you want. It's an amazing processor beyond any specifications you know. You want separation, that's what you will get. You are a powerful creator; you do not know this as yet. Your body wants something and the mind delivers. Your body says I want this, a reality of wanting develops, and an experience of wanting is given—no fulfillment, just an illusion. What you really need to live and develop is always provided. Without your asking, it comes your way. For your own reasons, you reject this and create your own wants and needs. The mind happily fulfills this and so you stay wanting, rejecting what you are given.

This is like saying I am given vegetables to eat and I want doughnuts and candy. Now, imagine if we reject vegetables and eat doughnuts and candy instead. I see it now, the consequence of this rejection and false acceptance. Now I get the picture you are trying to make me see. However, if you can balance the protein, carbs, fat, and sugar contents to align with what your body really needs, eating doughnuts and candy then becomes a normal situation. It's all about the balance and the use of protein, fat, carbs, and sugar to suit our body's need to grow. It's the same with the body-mind-soul combination; the use of all three in balance creates life in its real form that was meant to be. Now, this is an "Aha Aha!" moment.

Separation isolates everything from you like a shield, like a cloak. So you stay wanting in real life. To stay wanting and to need are two different situations. One is an expectation mode; the other is an execution mode. To be shown what you need, and accept and execute is what all of you must do. The difference between want vs. need is a choice you make as you go along. As of now, the want side of you is winning all the time. So you stay in the illusion, caught up from one want to another and to another in a never-ending loop. Life is a combination of all things present in your earth. Separation is just the opposite of life; it turns harmony and balance to chaos and imbalance. This is the way your world is today. It need not be and you can change this. Remove separation and embrace the Oneness. Shed the separation attitude. You don't need it and it does not unify your three aspects. Look to unify, not segregate your precious three aspects. Color is one way you separated yourself, but there are many other ways you created and adopted to separate—form, shape, language, region, country, thought, action, and so on; the list is endless. You are clever in creating items of separation because your mind is powerful to give you what you choose and want. This is giving you a false sense of power and making you believe this is real while this is just an illusion, a prop for you to play out. Just because a theater is set up and a play is acted out, it does not make it real. It still is an illusion.

Okay, I get it now. Let's take a computer or laptop analogy. Does the color of this hardware create hate? No, because all colored laptops work perfectly to their specifications regardless of their outer color. In this case, the color was just a choice. We are happy to take any color or a color of our preference. In the end, it works just the same. A white laptop or a black laptop with the same specs works exactly the same way. Now let's apply it to the human side. Aren't we all created the same? We have the same specs at birth. We have the same body parts, with a few differences like height and weight that we genetically inherited or acquired from our parents, having been born in different environments and in different human conditions. This makes us acquire different colors, forms, shapes, languages, and a host of other such external factors. Bringing the analogy of the laptop, we all have the same inbuilt specifications and we were all built to perform the same way. The only difference is that the applications loaded into each individual were and are different, and are based on each person's place of birth and the opportunities given to learn, play, work, and relax. Microsoft, Apple, Oracle, SAP, or any other such applications loaded onto any desktop or laptop, regardless of where it was bought or where the laptop owner lived, works the same way every time, everywhere. Can we not replicate this to give all humans the same application and the same opportunity that advanced countries give to their citizens and unify this world we live in? This will end separation to a large extent and begin the path to the oneness that we always had before us, but forgot to follow. All we need to do is remember. In this word lies a very powerful message. We were one before, separated at birth when we took physical form, waiting to rejoin and remember.

Judging human beings and segregating by outward appearances and external factors is rejecting them. This builds up separation. When you can do this in your mind, it becomes easy to carry separation and apply it to everything else. It becomes a habit and a second nature for all of you to judge outward visual differences and rank them. You are all different—not better, just different. Differences are valuable tools and a contextual field to see the opposite of you in human form. This is your teacher appearing once again to make you learn. You think of a teacher in human form; try seeing this in a non-human form. The learning here is meant to accept and use the contextual field to connect at the most basic level as two human beings. When this happens, a magic moment begins; when this is done collectively, a huge shift will start to take place. The energy that will be released will be so large that your present world will change to a new world for everyone to enjoy. Individual enjoyment never lasts; collective enjoyment never ends. That's how it works. The universe is waiting for this to happen.

Let's go back to history to see how this did not happen since 3500 BC. We have not learned from history. We still make the mistakes these civilizations made at a basic level. True, we have more advanced living comforts than these civilizations, but it's just body-enhancing comfort. Here are the last ancient eight broad civilizations: **Ancient African**—3000 BC to 1000 AD, lasted for 4,000 years;

Mesopotamia Empire—2270 BC to 695 BC, lasted for 1,575 years; **Ancient Indian Civilization**—2600 BC to 220 AD, lasted for 2,820 years; **Ancient Persia**—2240 BC to 224 BC, lasted for 2,016 years; **Ancient Chinese**—2100 BC to 220 AD, lasted for 2,320 years; **Ancient European**—2200 BC to 476 AD, lasted for 2,676 years; **Ancient Americas**—1200 BC to 200 BC, lasted for 1,000 years, and **Ancient Asian**—1200 BC to 668 AD, lasted for 1,868 years.

One of your archeologists came up with a civilization wave theory. The theory proposed a concept that a dominant form was always replaced by a lesser dominant form over a large time period by a cataclysmic event. The archeologist came to this conclusion after studying several historic ruins and sites. The archeologist was pointing humanity to a higher understanding. Dominance in any form is anti-evolution. Evolution favors continuity of life and will always dilute dominance. Evolution uses cataclysmic events to change the course and direct human and animal forms to a less-dominant way.

Yes, I remember reading this. The Ecuadorian archeologist was studying the Chicamocha warrior tribe and such other tribes in the Colombian valley. The study found that this dominant form was eventually replaced by the Inca civilization due to multiple cataclysmic tragedies. The study also noted that many such dominant forms all over South America, and possibly all over the world, followed this wave pattern. Just as the dinosaur, a dominant animal form, was wiped out by a cataclysmic event and replaced by smaller warm-blooded mammals with fur, evolution will always find a way to replace dominance. Dominant human and animal forms over millions of years have kept downsizing to less-dominant forms.

This is Evolution teaching you to become peaceful and to live in harmony and balance with all of life. Ask any of your historians, and they will tell you that the rise and fall of each of these civilizations can, in some way, be traced back to how they strived for dominance and how they lived as a community. A few people in each of these civilizations prospered, but the vast majority suffered and a selected few gained dominance. Prosperity and dominance for a few and poverty for everyone else were common elements in all of these civilizations. Natural cataclysmic disasters followed. War, poverty, disease, and natural disasters separated these people and slowly brought about the end of each of these civilizations. All of these are opposites to collecting, collating, and communalizing ways of life, embracing the ideology of oneness. All of you fractured your three aspects very early in your origin, and they remain fractured even today. Separation and dominance were the main root causes for all civilizations to fade away. This common thread runs through all of these civilizations as they rose in dominance and fell to cataclysmic disasters, to give way to lesser-dominant civilizations. Kings and kingdoms gave way to nations and democracy, a subtle way to dilute dominance and include all of life. You are not yet there, but you are slowly walking towards this direction. But now, you need to run.

It's been approximately 1,985 years since the death of Jesus Christ and 1,388 since the death of Prophet Mohammed, the last two prophets of Earth (35 AD and 632 AD). We are approaching the 2,000-year mark. Will we in this current form last? Will we—as the dominant form— survive? Let's try and evaluate. We have not yet given up our dominant ways. It is not as brutal as before, but it is still there. The world wars and the many other smaller wars only strengthen this argument. Will we in our current dominant form be replaced? Evolution is watching and waiting for us to change the course we are on today.

Your earth today has lost substantial topsoil, making crop cultivation very difficult going forward. Your ability to feed yourselves is rapidly diminishing. You have polluted your atmosphere; the crack in your ozone layer is widening. Microwave energy entering through this crack is melting ice at the poles. This will lead to seawater levels rising and lower seawater temperatures. This, in turn, will lead to flooding and the slow death of marine life, a natural disaster and the depletion of a valuable food source. This will also change the salinity of the seawater, causing colder temperatures, and ultimately—one day—the starting of an ice age. You are returning to where you started. Your inland water is shrinking. You are cutting down trees, shrinking the total forested area. This will decrease your nitrogen-oxygen ratio on earth. Soil, air, water, and trees are vital resources for human life to sustain. You are depleting and diminishing these valuable resources, while you continue to reproduce and grow in population. Evolution will make a decision soon to allow human life to continue or allow it to fade away and make way for another form of life, just as many other civilizations lived and died. This planet will survive beyond all of you; the question is, can you survive on this planet, the way you live now? Probably not the way you live now. You will end up depleting all of your resources and in doing so, slowly deny yourselves any chance to survive. History has not taught you anything so far. You still live the way civilizations in the past have, maybe in more comfort and pleasurable ways, and this makes you think you are advanced. Sadly, it's a big delusion. The comfort of the body without an accompanying contact with your soul is never a long-term sustainable path.

I am beginning to understand that cataclysmic events that wiped out earlier civilizations were evolution's way to change course—a sign and a reminder that the fundamental design element of life was violated, and natural laws broken. In this case, we are in pursuit and in favor of matter and material dominance. This is not sustainable. We have adequate natural resources, more than sufficient matter and material on this earth. Why add more if we do not know how to share this with everyone? We need to shed our violent ways, discard our violent thoughts, and live peacefully, including everyone and excluding no one.

This is true. Whenever the reproduction of human beings in peaceful, joyful, and loving environments is threatened, evolution will favor a change in life in the best interest of a higher purpose. This is how it is, and will always be for now and forever. The resources of your earth are being blatantly depleted; you could run out of them much sooner rather than later. If you do not accept and practice collecting, collating, and communalizing, reproduce and multiply to share and enjoy all of the resources with everyone, you will not be able to sustain and survive as a species. This is the fundamental and natural order of your universe. You have limited time. You need to speed up your process of personal and collective evolution before evolution charts its own course to correct. It's time to collect, collate and communalize the world. Hurry—you do not have much time.

How much time do we have? This is a question we all want to know and we probably will never know.

That's for all of you to come up with. It's your collective time on this earth. Will you make it or break it? It's for all of you to determine collectively, and ask if what you are doing is sustainable. If it is not, then why won't you change your ways? Human differences are meant to mix and blend your lives. Used well, they harmonize life. Weaponized, they turn out ugly and lead to conflict and violence. This is the attitude that is destroying you as a species, and you have not yet learned in millions of years that separation and dominance are the opposite of creation and life.

Yes, I agree, all of life is about creation. Ask any artist about this. He/she uses color, canvas, and brush to bring a painting to life. The use of the brush, color, and canvas creates harmony. It makes the painting come alive as the artist wants it to be. This is human creation at its best. There is no separation. The artist does not say, "I won't use black or white or brown colors." The artist is color neutral and uses all or any colors to enhance the painting. The artist naturalizes the painting to reflect what the artist wants to portray. A color is an option here made to create the painting, among many color choices available to the artist.

Life is all about using choices available to you on your earth to create and sustain for everyone. As the artist uses color, brush, and canvas to create broad brush strokes, use human differences to create broad strokes in life too. In doing so, you will end separation and begin creation. No life form, regardless of its outer appearance, is meant for segregation. Life is a gift, given to all of you to use in accumulation and to create harmony and balance.

A choice we don't make so easily. In fact, we need rules and laws to live. How about one simple way to live? Consider everyone and everything as one big family. So you are saying, what we do for our own family, do the same for the one big earth family?

Yes, why can't you do that? Using language and proper grammar, you create perfect sentences, stories, movies, and poetry; using musical notes, you create beautiful songs and melodies; using different colors, you create beautiful paintings. Why can't you create a beautiful life on your earth using all different life forms, humans, animals, trees, and plants in the way they came to earth and not the way you see them today in colors, forms, shapes, meat, and food? This is the alchemy of life. You need to understand this first and then accept it and finally live it.

Conflicts that happen in a family between siblings and parents are now happening on a global scale in the larger family of humans. We are unable to see beyond our smaller family, and we are also equally unable to keep our smaller family happy because our larger family is unhappy. Separation starts at our basic family unit and grows to engulf all of humanity. We are all one. We do not know this nor do we understand and accept this. It is but logical and natural that our smaller family can be happy only when our larger family stays happy.

Separation is non-life and leads to conflict. Ending separation is accepting life as it was given to you. The oneness of everything is the solution in today's troubled world. Your soul does not see or feel separated. It stays with you because it accepts you just the way you are. It goes away when you practice separation and make it your chosen path in your life, denying your soul any chance of creation experience. Birth is the start of your creative workshop, and death is the end of your chance and opportunity to keep the creative workshop open and running. Be wise and follow the natural law. Try and see the creator's signature in all living things and see how all of life is networked into one big universal chain. Plug into this vast resource, and experience who you really are—the product of an all-embracing oneness. This awareness will end separation and unite the world you live in. There is so much to see, so much to learn—why fight among yourselves for resources and things that belong to all of you?

When one day we understand that it's the larger family that counts, from that day onward, our smaller family will live in peace and joy. Until then, the struggle between what we want and what we really need will continue to grow.

Allow me to show you a passage that will sum it up:

"For I was hungry and you gave me to eat; I was thirsty and you gave me to drink; I was homeless and you found me shelter; I was naked and you clothed me; I was ill and you visited me; I was in prison and you brought me comfort. And everyone said, when did we see you hungry and feed you? Or thirsty and give you drink? And when did we see you homeless and find you shelter? Or naked and clothe you? And when did we see you ill or in prison and comfort you? And the answer that came was: Verily, verily, I say unto you—inasmuch as you have done it to the least of my people, my brethren, so have you done it to me."

This explains separation perfectly—there is no separation. Your suffering is mine too and your grief is ours too. We are all one large family.

Color

Chapter 3
The Dark Shadows
Cast from Differences

Another subject I spoke to my soul about was skin color. I said the soul has no color in a way we understand, but humans have, and why do we have so many skin colors and so many accompanying problems with it? This started our conversation. So here we go…

A biological efficiency created to compensate for a deficiency created by mass migration from warmer climates to colder regions became an issue for human ordination and subordination. Material possession cannot compensate for an evolutionary change. This created a whole new set of hierarchical disorders and disabilities that is so apparent today. We can try and explode the myth of melanin and pheomelanin that produces the white skin color and the collateral issues that came up to counter the absence of white color. From this point onwards, humanity took a different path that created a world full of differences with very little hope to reconcile. Your soul's color reflects and scatters all the visible colors, in the way you understand today. Physically, each of you has a single skin color at birth and so this could start a conversation, as you have.

I understand that white as a color saved those people who migrated from Africa to places which today we call Western Europe, the Americas, and Eastern Europe. This was a gift to all of them, a rare intervention to keep them living and multiplying. This was evolution's brilliance, turned into an ugly after-party fight by the very people who received the gift. The after-party fight began 8,000 years ago, and it shows no sign of ending. The big bang created only a bigger after-party fight.

The purpose of the big bang, as you say it, was to introduce life in its best form, evolving into a super form. What really happened is that the best form turned into a different form, with the differences growing sharper each millennium or every kilo year. You changed the direction and the intent of your creator and took it off-road into every sinkhole possible. You got all of life wrong, got the creator and the creation all wrong, and you marched along proudly like the Pied Piper of Hamelin with all of humanity following behind into the ocean of ignorance. The story and the tune of the Pied Piper of Hamelin was an illusion created for all of you to understand. Be aware and find a way to see through the illusion and accept the true reality. All of you happily dived into the illusion and made it your reality, while true reality sits in the middle, watching and waiting for you.

Color is a beautiful expression of nature. A golden sunset, a school of colorful fishes, a bunch of beautiful roses, a handful of orchids, white daffodils swaying in the breeze, the majestic peacock, clear blue skies, the lovely rainbow, the splendid white snowflake, the solid black leather sofa, the lush green grass, the grey winter sky, the emperor's royal dress, the chic black party gown, the spots on a leopard, and the stripes on a tiger. It's everywhere, and wherever you see color, you stand in awe at the sight of it on the ground, in the trees, on the animals, in the sky. However, when we see color in human beings, suddenly there is a different perception. The color one admired in nature is now despised and disrespected. This is so hard to understand.

Color on human skin has huge problems on today's earth. Let's see how the color on human skin evolved. Your own scientists have explained over the years how people from different parts of the world have different colored skin. People from the tropics generally have a darker skin color. Variations in human skin color are adaptive factors that evolved closely with the sun. As early humans moved into hot, open environments in search of food and water, one big challenge was keeping them cool. Since strong sun exposure damages the body, the solution was to evolve skin that was permanently dark so as to protect against the sun's more damaging rays. Melanin, the skin's brown pigment, is a natural sunscreen that protects tropical peoples from the many harmful effects of ultraviolet (UV) rays. UV rays can strip away folic acid, a nutrient essential to the development of healthy fetuses. Yet when a certain amount of UV rays penetrate the skin, it helps the human body use vitamin D to absorb the calcium necessary for strong bones. This delicate balancing act explains why the peoples that migrated to colder geographic zones with less sunlight developed lighter skin color. As people moved to areas farther from the equator with lower UV levels, natural selection favored lighter skin, which allowed UV rays to penetrate and produce essential vitamin D. The darker skin of people who lived closer to the equator was important in preventing folate deficiency.

In the words of the scientific community, skin color is primarily due to the presence of a pigment called melanin which is controlled by at least six genes. Both light and dark-complexioned people have melanin. However, two forms are produced—pheomelanin, which is red to yellow in color, and eumelanin, which is dark brown to black. People with light-complexioned skin mostly produce pheomelanin, while those with dark-colored skin mostly produce eumelanin. In addition, individuals differ in the number and size of melanin particles. The latter two variables are more important in determining skin color than the percentages of the different kinds of melanin. In lighter skin, color is also affected by red cells in blood flowing close to the skin. To a lesser extent, the color is affected by the presence of fat under the skin and carotene, a reddish-orange pigment in the skin. Hair color is also due to the presence of melanin. Melanin is normally located in the epidermis or outer skin layer. It is produced at the base of the epidermis by specialized cells called melanocytes.

These cells have photosensitive receptors, similar to those in the eye, that detect ultraviolet radiation from the sun.

Your scientists are correct in assuming this. Measures of skin reflectance—a way discovered by your scientists to quantify skin color by measuring the amount of light it reflects—in people around the world support this idea. While UV rays can cause skin cancer, and because skin cancer usually affects people after they have had children, it likely had little effect on the evolution of skin color. Evolution favors the continuation of life and adapts to make changes in your body over time to make reproduction the single most critical factor. Evolution favors changes that improve reproductive success. This is significantly important to understand in your discussion, the most important factor. When it comes to skin color, one of your scientific teams found a patchwork of evolution in different places and three separate genes that produce light skin, telling a complex story on how skin evolved to be much lighter during the past 8,000 years.

The modern humans who came out of Africa to originally settle in Europe about 40,000 years ago are presumed to have had dark skin, which is only advantageous in sunny latitudes. And new data confirms that about 8,500 years ago, early hunter-gatherers in Spain, Luxembourg, and Hungary also had dark skin.

Color is part of your evolution, a natural selection process, not an original human specification that your creator fashioned. It is a part of your walk from Africa to what you now call Europe and to America. You were all dark 8,000 years ago. Lighter skin, or what you call white skin, evolved in the last 8,000 years. Evolution found a way to protect human reproduction and maintain human life on earth, by keeping dark skin for people who stayed back near the equator and lightening the skin for people who migrated to colder climates. You have got color all wrong. There is no rank order of color. It was evolution—protecting the human ability to reproduce—preserving folic acid and essential vitamin D for reproductive success.

From this truth, many lies were born and over many years, color was weaponized. Today, color stands abused.

What evolution did to maintain, preserve, produce and sustain; all of you used to malign, put down, rank and judge other humans and take advantage of a natural process of evolution. Color is purely relational to show differences in people living in colder and hotter climates—nothing more and nothing less. People don't evolve; species evolve over a long period of time. White color, as you call it, evolved over a very long period. Dark color was the original selection, the original design element. As many of you started moving out of Africa to colder places, evolution found a way to adapt to low sunlight and cold by lightening the skin to allow and adapt to fewer UV rays, increase folic acid and vitamin D, allow human reproduction, and grow the human population. Without folic acid and vitamin D, humans are unable to reproduce. This is the truth. If you understand this, it will set you free from prejudice, bias, and judgment, for all humanity to stay connected and be one large family. Separation is never in your best interest and does not serve your purpose. Collect, collate and communalize is your best way forward.

Groundbreaking DNA analysis revealed that the first modern Briton had dark skin and blue eyes. London scientists said this on Feb 7, 2018, based on their findings. They found that the lighter pigmentation of the Northern European population is more recent than previously thought. The man who lived 10,000 years ago was brought to life through the first-ever full DNA analysis of his remains. The skeleton discovered in Southwest England in a cave was known as the Cheddar Man, named after the area. In a joint project between Britain's Natural History Museum and University College London, scientists drilled a 2 mm hole into the skull and extracted bone powder for analysis. Their findings showed the Cheddar Man had blue eyes and really dark skin, contradicting the earlier version of brown eyes and light skin. A Briton, 10,000 years ago, having blue eyes and dark skin surprised Chris Stringer of the museum, who for the past decade has been analyzing bones found in the same cave.

Reproduction is a critical design element for life to sustain, maintain, and evolve. A human being was created in the highest design specification, meant to live, produce, sustain, evolve, and go on forever. Your ancient scripture tells you, "Go forth and multiply." You did your part to multiply, and evolution did its part to sustain all of you, as you walked the earth and moved and lived in all corners, far and wide. You were abundantly provided with natural resources to maintain this growing human population. This was creation at its highest form. Sadly, you never distributed the abundant resources around. Man kept what was in his backyard; nations kept what belonged inside their border. The opportunity to share was lost. Separation was born, and you lost your way.

My conversation on color is an ongoing struggle to bring to the surface the dark shadows built over 8,000 years on skin color. We have given it too much relevance, made it overly significant. This is nothing but fake news and fake perception. In my opinion, in the world of flowers, does color make the white lily hate the black/red rose? No. Both live in harmony, glorifying each other, growing from the same earth and nurturing themselves to full bloom, making people happy. Did the blue sky turn on the dark sky? No. Both lived and came on without conflict. In the world of humans, why is color so relevant? We made this up, we built it up, we hyped it up and we promoted it and took it beyond proportion to serve our narrow interests. We always find a way to glorify our differences because it suits us to stay dominant over others. Once again, separation and dominance is the path we choose, just as our ancestors did.

Again, you are promoting separation. It is observed that while inanimate objects of color are appreciated and animal life forms with color are loved, a human being with color is despised. What logic is there in this way of perception? White and black are opposites meant for contrasting and for understanding as opposite spectrums. Without the black, you can never understand white. Without the white, you would only know black. It is just a way to expand your understanding of two colors, not a way to create an up or down vote. This is your teacher and your teaching, and the wisdom you have never truly understood. A classroom is really not needed to learn. Teaching can come from experiencing life. Every moment you are provided opportunities to learn; all you need to do is simply observe, learn, and grow.

When darker-skinned people were enslaved and brought from warmer climates to slavery in colder climates, I think a natural law was violated. The dark-skinned people's natural habitat changed. The bringing of dark-skinned people to the west was purely to fill a large gap in farm labor—incorrect use of human resources. It was like moving a tropical animal like the tiger to the North Pole. Will it survive? Probably not, but nature will find a way to adapt and probably make minor changes in the tiger's external body to adapt, shed its stripes, and take on white skin.

Human beings have never understood the world you live in. What damage you do to life, evolution finds a way to repair and allow the species to live and reproduce. This is the very highest and purest form of creation and design. Life must go on, even if it means external mutations over time. Changes are made for an entire species to survive, never meant for an individual. This is what all of you have never understood. The struggle between being strongly individual and the desire to be strongly collective has been the human struggle over thousands of years. The individual is winning and the collective is losing. This is a failure in epic proportions. Unless all of you reverse this trend, long-term survival is in danger.

So it was never meant for the white man to blow his trumpet on his skin color, nor for the black man to use arrows to kill the white man trumpeting. No one is higher than the other, they are just different. Without the white skin color, the white man and his white woman could never have produced children. Without the black skin color, the black man and his black woman could also have produced no children. All of Africa would be today without people and all of West would be barren empty land. This did not happen, but it could have.

Yes, evolution found a way to adjust and compensate for the sun's UV rays and preserved folic acid and vitamin D to maintain reproduction, by lightening the skin color. This is the truth. From this truth, many lies were born, many stories created. Dominance, separation, and slavery took shape and form, bloomed and sustained themselves. Today you see the after-effects of this distortion.

Color is a human thing. It's a physicality. Judgment made on color is also a human thing, born from a lack of understanding. When we know and understand this as the truth, it should set us free, because we should know that what was created was the long-term continuation of life to sustain our species. What we did not know is this fundamental truth. We never embraced and accepted this fact. We grew up materially and religiously, never intelligently. Our ancestors millions of years ago never saw color. They were all dark, and their only concern was hunger and survival. Since these are no longer issues today in most places, we see color. What was done to protect against the sun has now turned a human being against another. I see a white man and a woman walking, he sees a black man and a woman running—these are stories we humans created. This is a comic book story. In reality, there are only four people. The color was a conversation we brought to life for no reason. It's time to take it away, get this elephant out of the room.

Yes, it's about time, you did this. How much longer do you need to nurse this grudge?

Let me bring up the story of Adam and Eve. In the story, they didn't see nakedness until they ate the fruit, and then, they saw it. One can argue and debate whether the *serpent* was the culprit or if the *fruit* was too tempting, or if *Eve* was weak. All three are perceptions. We can blame any of the three or choose one of the three to judge and condemn. We took the easy path to condemn Eve and blame Adam. To judge another was a very early trait. It then became a way forward. What could have happened that could make more sense, as I see it, was that both saw and understood the nakedness of a male and a female body? The visual and mental cortex synchronized to understand nakedness as a state of being, seen by a male and by a female as the first humans, and the opportunities it provided.

Sex was born, a child was born, and the rest is history.
This is first birth as you claim it to be, not really fully true.
There were many others, but let's stay with it, and for the
first time, the first woman understood sex as an opportunity
to bear children and the first man became aware for the first
time of his opportunity to have sex and the ability to raise a
family. There was no one to tell or advise them. This was
how early humans learned about life, from the moment and
from the present. It is so sad to see that today, you do not
live in the moment and in the present and, therefore, so
many opportunities presented are lost.

In the same way when hunger and survival that kept us together as hunter-gatherers vanished, due to the abundance of food grown and produced, we suddenly saw color as another state of being. Visibility is a function of the eye; however, if the image is not processed in our brain, we are unable to give it a meaning. When we overcame hunger and survival, we forgot our common ancestry and the fact that when many of us walked out of Africa in search of food and shelter to colder climates, our skin started to change color. If this is a fact, why don't we accept it?

Evolution is clever, it adapted to protect human life in
colder climates to allow reproduction of the species. It
simply changed skin color over the years, to keep your folic
acid and vitamin D intact. The point is when one part of
your physical self-sufficiency is achieved, another
deficiency becomes visible, and another illusion is born.
Your ancestors never observed that changes made were
design changes. Due to the geographical changes you made,

a simple adjustment was made to allow you to sustain life. You were so happy in that state that you forgot the skin color changes taking place. This is just a sign of you, being a young species in this vast universe, or shall we call it multiverse? You are doing well, slowly evolving. Look at how much progress you have made from your cave times and know this—that you are still far away from your true potential to be a Highly Evolved Being. The fact that you are asking and talking about this only means you are awake and want to be fully awake.

Yes, that is our destination, but it looks so far away. Right now, we need to understand that human differences in physicality are life's teaching tools that we must come together. If we see differences differently, then we lose the opportunity to grow and develop.

The differences are a contextual field so that you may understand white from black, light from darkness, cold from heat. So use this wisely to grow and evolve to a higher level. How else can you describe cold if you never experience heat? The field of opposites is a tool for you to know the difference and more importantly to understand the difference and use it to raise yourselves to the next higher standard. If you focus too much on the items of difference, you are bound to lose focus on the purpose of it being made contextual. Heat or cold, light or darkness, white or black are not things to choose but to understand that an opposite pair is brought into reality for you to know and learn. Just like that, the opposite appears as a teacher. Instead of learning, you start to attack the teaching, only because it is a differently-held belief from your commonly-held understanding. It's a violent nature of your humanity that is built on the survival instinct. The classroom moment is gone, the battlefield moment begins. It's an instinct that does not serve you well today. If you cling on to survival as an instinct, violence is an accessory you cannot shake off. It becomes accompanying baggage, an accessory that comes along.

To overstress the good and condemn the bad takes away this learning opportunity. Both need to exist for us to make our choice. I understand this. We also need to understand that both opposites are brought into reality for us to learn that living together with the opposite in harmony uplifts our higher aspect. This is why good and evil exist in the same place. Not to live well is evil.

Without evil, how will you ever understand the goodness of good? The appearance of the opposite is a lesson for learning. You never understood this as a human race. The Pied Piper of Hamelin's tune is too strong for you to break your march to the river. Eventually, after many wars and tragedies, after destruction and famine, after climate changes, earthquakes and floods, you will finally learn to live in peace, joy, and love. Catalytic events are simply learning points to understand that you are self-creating the disaster by the choices you make. You are not the victim here and looking for the villain to blame is denial. Remember what you deny controls you. Using violence and anger to resolve life's most basic issues is not the path to development.

Yes, violence is now a part of us. It has trailed us since we walked out of the jungle to the cities we now live in. It still continues to stalk us. Take grammar in any language— there are rules to follow. If we follow the rule, the sentence comes out well and acceptable. Similarly, I think, human differences were created in the same way to use them wisely to create harmony. Just as we need a verb, an adjective, a noun, and so on to create a sentence that can be understood, we need to use human differences to create a collective life that can be meaningful. A verb and an adjective have nothing in common yet put together, they become meaningful. Let's give the verb color white, the adjective color black and the noun color brown. Put all of them together wisely and you get perfect life.

This is what you need to replicate, use human differences to create a perfect life for all of you to live in harmony.

No single note in music is the same. They are all different. When put together, they create a beautiful tune, a beautiful song. When we hear this beautiful song, do we hear the different notes or do we just hear the tune, the melody, and the song?

It's the same. Use human differences to create a life melody. The mixing of everything and everyone is the grand recipe for life to evolve. If you focus on individual elements, you forget the full majesty of life. In all of life, there is unity and harmony. Try and see it.

I can see how the mountain lives peacefully by the river and how the sky and the sun live in harmony, how plants and trees live with the animals, supporting each other, nurturing each other. Only a human lives in conflict with another human. We need to observe and adapt.

Only when violence is taken out of your lives will human beings as a species survive and develop. Survival is meaningless if you haven't grown. Technology is useless if you have not evolved. Violence is a primitive way to resolve any conflict. Color today has enlisted itself as one reason to become violent. I agree, let's change this conversation and take color out of your lives.

As I understand, the white man is our brother from Africa, who moved away from home thousands of years back. The black man is our original family that stayed back in Africa. The white woman is our sister from Africa who went with the man to start a new family. Over time, their skin turned white to compensate for UV rays, allow reproduction, and avoid annihilation. It's just one big family. No one remembers this anymore.

All you need to do is remember. All you need to do is remember and re-member with your world family living everywhere. Let not skin color infect your ability to understand higher things. This thinking will continue to incubate and infect you until you make skin color irrelevant to life. Life is so much more than just skin color.

Possession

Chapter 4
The Costs of Serving Only
the Needs of Body and Mind

Can we talk about possession? I think it is a branch of
separation and a concept that has survived since life began
on earth. It remains until today, a very essential and vital
part of human life. None of us has ever understood the idea
that we were born with no possessions, just the ability to
create and call for whatever experiences we want in life. So
if we were born with no possessions, what is making us
want to possess and own anything and everything? The
answer lies in the creation of money and the concept of
dominance and separation. When was money created?
Money, in some form, has been part of human history for
the last 3,000 years. It started as a need to barter goods, to
give what we have in surplus and to get things that we did
not have. Confined to this need-based state, this barter was
a good concept. However, over the years, this concept
rapidly leaped upward to create an extreme surplus for some
and extreme deficit for others. Poverty and abundance were
born as twins. The more money was created, the less of it
others got. Need-based demand gave way to wealth in

excess of need for some and for many, the struggle began to acquire wealth. Possession started by announcing what was mine is mine and I will protect it from the rest. The have-nots resorted to stealing and the haves took to arms to protect.

I think you are onto something. What was once a need was twisted out of shape to something else. As wealth accumulated beyond need, this excessive wealth led to the production of goods and services for consumption and the capitalist republic was born. Take a look at what was created; just matter, material and services—all serving the needs of the body and ego of the mind. This triggered the need as seen today for possession. It is natural that if you have an excess of things, you need to protect them and the more you protect them, possession as an idea grows in size and proportion inside all of you. Today, it is too complex to de-link possession from your lives. Over thousands of years, possession expanded its scope. Starting from incense, land, and gold, it grew exponentially as wealth grew. Today the list just keeps increasing to add on pets, houses, extended families, alternate families, cars, jets, boats, islands—the list is endless. Possession has today become a critical element of your life. It seems all of you work and struggle to raise income and add wealth to own and spend and then pay down what you borrowed to own, all your life. With this comes along service providers, material providers, and dream providers—as you call it—to provide materials, services, and dreams you crave. The cycle never ends; your cravings never stop. You have practically invented new needs. Now ask yourself if any of the current needs you have created over centuries fulfills this one true need? Sadly, all of your actions in the past and present were and are in the opposite direction.

It is so clear now that over many years, we have added new needs to use borrowed wealth and excessive wealth we created for ourselves. Now I see where money has taken us in the wrong direction. To protect possessions, nations have gone to war, families have gone into conflicts, siblings have killed to claim and reclaim possession in the name of "give me back what was mine." We have all gone nuts wanting to own and then protect what we own and, if necessary, fight and kill to reclaim what we lost.

It is time to give up possessions because it has become a horrible struggle for all of humanity, for the rich and the poor alike. Earth in all its splendor was given to all of you to share and rejoice in. There are no registration desks in heaven—a place you call paradise—to record ownership. Ownership is a human element born from greed and excessive needs. Remember the ancient saying, "I am my brother's keeper and my sister's protector?" You are all brothers and sisters from the same higher being, born differently in different places with the same human specifications, yet all of you do not as yet have the collective wisdom to become a global community. In such a given environment, one does not need private ownership.

While this is a good idea, many people see this as socialism, a part of communist ideology that never worked.

The problem with that logic is that communism and socialism were forced upon people, against their will. What we are talking about is people willingly agreeing to share and inviting everyone to enjoy in a loving and peaceful way. This is so different from what you call socialism. The haves and the have-nots join together to make a community of all haves. In such a community, possession is an unknown concept. It's time to stop making excessive wealth and creating additional needs. It's about time to share the abundant resources that were placed at the disposal of all humanity. It was dispersed across all far corners of the world, only to allow all of you to come together, like what you call a pound party. Bring a pound of a dish from your home to share with one another at another home. Everyone gets to taste the best of everyone. That's an idea worth pursuing on a global scale. What all of you do in your individual homes and in smaller communities is so beautiful; why you can't do this on a larger scale with your larger family spread all over the earth is so difficult to understand.

We did this in a movie, "Independence Day" in 1996 and a sequel in 2016. All of the earth's communities came together to join in the fight against the alien starship. There was communication between every nation on earth. All had a unified purpose to save the earth.

Are you saying you need an alien invasion or a cataclysmic event to happen for all of humanity to come together? You mean the threat of extinction has to be made real before all of you wake up? Can't you see the signs slowly unfolding right in front of you? Why do you have to wait until the eleventh hour to spring into action?

This is a concept that is so hard to understand and even harder to get everyone to participate in and practice, but we must try and start soon. I am getting to understand that to share is creation at its best, while to own and protect is separation at its worst. If I ask myself, was the earth created in its full majestic splendor for one to own any or all parts of it? I would have to say no because it didn't come with a title or titles. We gave it titles. This is a human thing. To share the beauty of this earth and allow the sharing, to bring joy, peace, and love is something we need to do.

So then hurry up, this is what your soul wants and is looking for and you keep denying it for your own reasons. Your soul needs nothing from you, just the experience of you being in harmony with all of life, enjoying all of life and sharing with all of life. You are all one, dismembered at birth, waiting to be re-membered. Give up the need to possess and see what lies beyond. You have everything to give because you have the ability to create joy, peace, and love on this earth you live in. Possession is just the opposite direction of where you should be going.

We do not know this as yet. I feel we will one day, but it may be too late, as we continue endangering our earth and continue to possess, separate, fight, and isolate ourselves. There is nothing to possess; it's all freely available, just share it with everyone and enjoy living on earth. To possess is to deny another. Isn't this separation at its best form? See how possession leads to separation? Separation will one day bring all of us to the endpoint, an end we are engineering ourselves. It's not too late to change course. Walk away from possession and keep separation far away. Don't we all practice this with our children? We share our things with them and live in peace. Why is this not scalable to the large human family? Within our family, we embrace this concept; outside our family, we oppose it. Isn't this separation? What does one need to unify a simple loving way of life within a universal family of everyone? Color, separation, and possession are human characteristics that disable our growth and prevent us from seeing a bigger picture and being a bigger person. This is like living in a well with tunnel vision. We become unable to see the wide world.

Color, separation, and possession are linked; one leads to another. The cocktail is deadly and evolution will not allow this to happen. It will alter the course if you do not alter your ways. What you don't understand and accept today is the definition of the family. Just because a child was born to you and raised by you does not make the child your possession and make your family waterproof. Your child is not born in isolation. You and your child will live and grow with everyone else. So how can you practice separation and possession, when your family depends on everyone else, and the more others are enriched, the more your child will be enriched? Taking possession of matter and material only for you, for your family, and for your child teaches him/her to do this, as he/she grows up to become an adult. What are you passing on—values or just matter and material? Think about it carefully. You know very well and you practice it well too, the concept of sharing within a family. All you need now is to work harder to expand its scope to include all of the human family. One day, you will know that in the deepest sense, all of you are all one—you come from the same being, from the same energy source and that makes this world what it is.

Our sense of visual identity works against us. What we cannot see, we cannot relate to. This stops us from using our soul to understand such concepts. So I say, hey! Bring the soul into this partnership and let's work as a body-mind-soul partnership. This will allow us to see the universal signature of pure creation in everything. We should be able to see all of life. We are the singular aspect of the one big aspect. We are the plurality of that singularity, the seven billion on earth.

As an individual person, when you see the universality of everything, possession will no longer be relevant. All you need is to plug into the network and enjoy the abundant resources. The World Wide Web was created to pass on a valuable lesson—what we share grows for everyone. We took the creation of the web to enrich ourselves and forgot the bigger lesson. The network is big and you are part of it like everyone else. Add to the web for everyone to enjoy. Does the web and the internet of things belong to anyone in particular? No. Plug in, log in and browse happily. Duplicate this in all other aspects of life. The title of matter and material is a smaller concept. Living, experiencing, and expressing from the benefits of the universal plug-in is far more valuable and a sustaining life event, meant to prolong and produce. Go ahead and make yourselves individually important; also make everyone else equally important. Complete the circle of life. In a circle, all things along the circle are equal and so, make it so in life too.

So what you are saying is from a **small** ME, become a **bigger** ME, and then become a **universal** ME!

Yes, all of life is waiting for this to happen. This alone can change the world you live in, and change you must if you need to survive as a human race. Evolution is watching and waiting to see if you can accelerate and develop. Take all the help you want, call for it and accept it, but please, move on.

The Villain and the Victim
Chapter 5
A Vicious Human Cycle
We Must Stop

We are moving on to another subject that follows the possession trail into the wilderness. Too much of possession takes us to this wild jungle where the mighty rule and the not so mighty fall prey. Yes, this is the world of the villain and the victim; the place where the villain becomes the victim and then changes to become a villain

All of you attach yourselves to one of the two characters in every situation of life. You are the villain or the victim and at times both. To most of you, it seems, either you have been victimized or you have villainized others. These two states of mind have not allowed you to evolve—how can you? You are carrying unnecessary baggage, you stand separated, you cling on to your possessions, and you seek justice for everything that goes wrong. Isn't it but natural to fall into one of the two categories? It only seems logical that this happens. Reacting traps you into one of the two victim-villain isolation chambers.

I see what you mean. It is our way of thinking that has brought this about. Since we carry a lot of unwanted baggage we don't need, and which others need badly, we are opening ourselves to be victimized. Having been victimized, we become villains to reclaim what is lost.

Do you see the irony and the dichotomy? You picked up stuff you don't want, then you do not share this with others who need it. Finally, you shout "Hey, I was robbed, now I am the victim here, I just got taken." What kind of sense does this make? To make matters worse, you ask for and seek revenge and become a villain. Nicely done, become a victim, then become a villain. Don't you see this cycle that keeps moving like a figure eight, up and down these two character lanes, in a loop forever?

I understand justice can never be a reaction; it should be an action. A reaction is the opposite of creation. Nothing new is being created, only the past experience replicated. When justice becomes an action, it bypasses the villain/victim track. Since we are inserting justice in what we do, ahead of the event, that causes injustice, nothing bad comes from this. So there is no need for anyone to become a victim and no need to assume a villain position. This way, we have created justice in what we do and not reacted to seek justice from what just happened.

Yes, creation overcomes many issues at the starting point, eliminating any need to react. Reaction is mainly a human issue. It exists in the absence of creation and grows rapidly to overtake and become your leading character trait, a behavior that ultimately masks and reduces your ability to create. If you overcome this, justice as an action becomes a creative effort, dissolving the need for revenge. Now you can see once again that creation resolves many of your problems ahead of time.

It's like creating a safe passage on the road you travel, for yourself and for others. Suddenly, it becomes a superhighway where everyone is cruising along happily. A road full of happy drivers seldom has an accident to report. No loss of life, no loss of limbs, and no loss of property, simply because we consciously created this. Where is the need for justice now? It has suddenly become an action in your creation.

All of life is simple. It's you who have made it complex, and then you need to have complex thoughts to understand the complexity you just made. Take away this human concept of looking at life from your point of view and life becomes simple. Look at it in totality in a collective way. Make it simple for the other person and he or she will make it simple for you and both of you can cruise along. Stop thinking inside this victim/villain box. It will only keep you inside this box. Think differently and the box will expand into a wide universe. Your soul can help you do this; your body cannot do this, and your mind is too addicted to the body and not helpful. It's your body that is demanding possessions, then asking the mind for protection, and then using the mind to plan revenge for injustice. Ask your soul for help to change the way you think and you will no longer be victimized or become a villain to re-possess.

So our soul needs nothing from us and demands nothing from us. All that is being asked is the experience of who I really am—a creative being with the ability to create and express joy, peace, and love, avoiding violence and conflict in my life and in other lives too.

Yes—when you create, you touch other people and when they create, it touches you. This is the circle of life. In this circle, there are no victims or villains—never can be. You have just lifted yourself from what you were to what you want to be. This is creation at its very best. You are a perfect being. You just don't know this as yet or you haven't remembered it fully. You are neither a victim nor a villain; your thinking has made you believe this. It's an illusion, a contextual field for you to see the reality of who you are in the victim/villain scenario.

This is like a video game; play and move to the next stage. So you are saying, without this contextual field we would never know the real us and if we stay in the game, the illusion becomes our reality; but if you play it knowing that it's a game and you have a purpose to play it in the way you are expected to, you then will ace the game. There are no victims or villains in real life, it's just an illusion for us to see what's at play and what we need to do. We need to look at it as our canvas to paint what we need, not what we want.

Like any game, keep moving to the next level and deal with the situation that helps you to move ahead, never forgetting who you are. You are not a character in the game of life. You are an outsider playing the game, and the characters appearing on your game screen are generated to give you a field of play. If you get too personal with the character, you are going to stay in the game and struggle to get to the next level and complete the game. A good gamer knows this; he or she deals with the situation with the tools he/she has and with the objective to move to the next level. All of life is very similar. From birth to death, you come across multiple characters in the form of parents, siblings, friends, colleagues, and strangers. What's your strategy here? Get too personal? Of course, you can. You stop by in a game to chat up with someone you like, and sure, something will come out and attack you. So too in life chat up, but keep your mind sharp on what your true objective is and move to a higher level, dealing with the situation and the characters in a manner that is helpful for you and for them. When you help someone else to go where they want to go, will there be any chance to become a villain or a victim? I don't think so. Now, justice has become an action, not a reaction.

Are you saying that because all of us are the same beings, incarnated in different forms and in different environments, we now have a wide gaming field to play with everyone?

Play well and move on. Never leave someone behind, never hurt anyone, never be violent, and respect all you meet. This will help you move up to your next level. Without another, how can you move anywhere? A set of opposites have to come in front of you to allow you to choose. Without *the opposite appearing as a context, you will never know your next move or your next choice.*

That makes a PC, playing a character in a game and an NPC, *non-playing character* in a game two examples of opposites in any game. While the NPC is just a distraction to slow us down, the PC is our main opposition or your friendly help, depending on the game. Understanding each of them is our task and our prime objective. We need to engage with them in a purposeful way and move on.

Yes—in life too, you will come across NPCs and PCs, as you term them. Both appear to give you a contextual and a perceptive field. In this field, you will discover your true self if you deal with the PCs and NPCs calmly, respectfully, and peacefully. They help you in your quest, as long as you do not get absorbed with their personalities. If you do, the illusion becomes stronger, taking you off your main track. You can do this—there is no obligation, no compulsion. Take your time to play in a different reality. The journey just gets longer, but what's the hurry? There are hundreds of lifetimes available to start again from where you left off.

Creation builds life upwards. This should be our operating motto. In doing so, the words victim and villain disappear from our world, simply because we created justice ahead of anything, avoiding the need to seek justice as a follow-up. Our thoughts make us what we become. Our deed follows our thought, our action follows our deed, and consequences follow our action. So if our sponsoring thought is not justice for all, then our action and the resulting consequence moves into the victim-villain environment. This routine only creates more sub-routines like conflict, anger, violence, killing, etc. We can easily eliminate all of this from our Gaya field and from our U-shadow, two science fiction artificial intelligence concepts that can become a reality when artificial intelligence starts to expand and engulf all of our current technology. Gaya field and U-shadow are virtual perceptions, created as holographic images to assist you in evaluating your local situation and to give you the best of information and intention in making a safe decision to deal with and pass through. While technology can aid and improve our life, what use is this when our sponsoring thought is not justice? All of the technology used well with the sponsoring thought of justice for all can help to take our world away from the villain and victim torture chambers.

You are the intelligence. You don't need artificial intelligence; just use your natural intelligence. In true reality, there are no villains and victims. Your thinking has created this. How can there be any victims, if you want to share everything with everyone? How can there be any villains when there is no need to steal, lie, or take away things because everything now is available to you as a shared resource? When this becomes a universal practice, then in one moment, your world will transform into a different reality. It takes very little to do this, but it is so hard that millions of years have passed and yet, you are nowhere close. In fact, your need to own and possess is deeply rooted in your basic instinct for survival. This instinct is no longer relevant and has no purpose in your current life stage. Survival and xenophobia are now glowing human characteristics that are slowing down your path to evolve to the next level. All of you are well past the survival instinct, but you still cling to it, because it makes you warm and comfortable. You have stayed in this area for so long that you have made this instinct your comfort blanket, warm and snug.

So villain and victim are twins, born from excessive obsessional needs, as a way to showcase our separation and dominance, which is rooted in our attitude. All of this is intertwined and interlinked to take us far away from who we really are. These are just illusions and road markers to show us how far away we are in the opposite direction. So there is no need to despise them. Take them as learning points to recommence our walk in the opposite direction from where we are now. All of this is excessive baggage we really don't need and it is costing us a dear lot in holding on to this. We don't need this baggage. Don't check this baggage in on our flight to the next higher level. We need to empty it out in our neighborhood garbage bin, or in our city recycle station. Check-in without all of this to take a freedom flight to the next frontier of human civilization— a free unified land for all and a glorious life for everyone, for we are not separate—just different aspects of the one true reality. That is all there is and that which always will be for now and forever. It's time to go home or come home.

Yes, the universe is waiting for you to take your next step and is helping you in ways you do not understand and do not see. You can also ask for help from your soul. Be wise, seek help, and elevate yourself. This is your moment. Allow it to come to you.

The Illusion

Chapter 6
A Tool and a Teacher
for Us to Awaken

We are born and we die. We came from somewhere and we go back somewhere.

All forms must eventually end; that is the way of every form. Now energy is a different matter; it can never be created nor destroyed, but it can create forms. A form is temporary, a transition from creation to re-creation, and this is what you call birth and death.

As I see it, birth is an acronym for *Begin Re-creation Transit Human*. Death is an acronym for *Delink Energy and Transit Human*. Birth is a transition from spirit form to a physical form and death is the transition from physical form back to spirit form. We don't really die; we simply change our form. The in-between is what we understand as life on earth. Now we do not see the in-between period as an illusion because, for us, it appears real. In reality, it is a prop to enable us to know who we really are, but we have made the illusion our reality.

That was clever to create and expand the acronym, but they are just words. You need to go deeper than expanding acronyms. An energy source that materialized in human form will dematerialize in spirit form at the end, sometime. Creation and re-creation, that's what you need to take away.

It's just like being inside the game of Jumanji. Everything appears real and feels real. How you move to the next level depends on how you act and interact at the moment and how many lives you have. It's the same in the universe. We have many lives, we die and are born again. The only difference is we are born young and die old. It's the same concept. What we do NOW at this moment will take us to the next level.

Literally, you are shaping your tomorrow by your today and you have three tools: your body, your mind, and your soul. How well you use them and how synchronized you keep all three together is your individual choice, and this is your real freedom. Your will cannot be thwarted, because your will is the creator's will. It's the freedom you all have to live your life the way you want to.

So individual self-development plans without the collective development plan are self-defeating simply because we are not separate beings. We are individual beings forming a community to declare, express and experience the singularity in all of us, smaller parts of a larger part. We are proud to be different, ashamed to be alike. What a way to live?

Whenever you interact in life with just one aspect from your three aspects, the story and the picture rolls out differently. If you use just your body, you get a different experience, and when you use too much of your mind, you get a different experience, and when you use the mind-body combination, you get a totally different experience. Finally, when you use your body-mind-soul combination to guide you, it's a whole new experience. The realities keep changing when you change, adapt, and use these tools in singularity, duality, or in plurality. You come across situations differently in each of the paths you follow. There is nothing wrong or right here, it is what it is. So if you lose track of what you were born for, you will keep experiencing everything differently in this lifetime and every lifetime until you finally get the message.

Are you saying, each one of us is creating different situations based on how each of us is using our three tools? Since we all live together, these situations affect each of us in different ways. Just as in the game when we play a certain way, the game situation changes, our lives change as we make our own choices and decisions. If the gamer forgets his end goal to reach the highest level using the tools the game gives, then the end becomes impossible and the struggle gets harder.

It is the same in life. Your highest level is to experience, express, and declare who you really are and live life in this experience. In your core, you are nothing but love, peace, and joy. This is your goal and the highest level. Nothing else matters. Everything else is a distraction, just an illusion.

That is an understanding we haven't fully understood. Our filter is still very thick. In life, as in any game, we will meet NGCs—non-game characters meant to distract us. If we engage with them too long, our move to the next level will be that much harder. If we can keep this as our core objective, we should be able to move through life lovingly, joyously, and peacefully.

When you do this and your neighbor does this and your partner, your friends, and everyone on earth, you will have created a great experience for all of you to move through. You all have to move together, just like a train with all its cars coupled to your end destination. Here is my question: What's the purpose of going to the endpoint without anybody? This is where you lose your sense of being collective and become individuals, far too individualistic.

This understanding will change the way you live today and bring in peace and harmony tomorrow. You do not have to wait millions of years more to understand this. You can— right now—change your world. All of life is a grand illusion, a contextual field that props up when you interact in a particular way and changes when you change your way. You are the creator and the gamer moving through people, places, and objects to reach your end goal. To express and experience who you really are, you use all of the three aspects in balance, in harmony, respecting each aspect for the purpose it was designed for. Built in you is an internal guidance system that is designed to tell you your truth and bring you home. And know it now, that your soul is your guidance system—what you call on earth a GPS—your life's navigational guidance tool. Use it well.

I get it. GPS alone gets us nowhere. We need a car, gas, and a driver to use the GPS. I can see now how different things are needed to achieve my goal. In life, we need everything and everyone to help us move through.

*Life is creating a path forward for you to move, but if you think the situation in front of you is real, engage with it. Should you do so with your earth-acquired personality, you will get stuck at this level and struggle to reach your next level. While the struggle is good, it is also a teacher, teaching you that the path you are now on is not the correct path. It's time to switch paths. Learn from the struggle; do not curse your fate. Fate, after all, is **For All Thoughts Everywhere**. Fate, in reality, is collective actions affecting you, happening in your neighborhood. You can be a part of this, or parts of this can be affecting you. Move away from this path if this is causing you issues. Choose another neighborhood. Cursing this environment is not going to help you. Move on, find another path to walk on. Accept the teaching, understand the struggle, listen to the teacher, and change your course. Life is showing you a way out of the situation.*

So we need to consider the illusion as our prop, a scene, a stage on which we go through life, but respect it for it is our way forward, and treat everything and everyone respectfully as we navigate through it, never forgetting our end goal and our highest level, as told to us.

This is your purpose in life. Don't take the illusion too seriously. If you do, it then becomes your reality. Remember your poetry, "You have miles to go and things to do before you die." What it really means is, move through your today with love, peace, and joy and experience the highest form of your true feeling before your life ends. The illusion is a tool, a teacher, helping you to get to the reality; nothing more and nothing less. Don't take the illusion seriously; use it wisely to move forward. The illusion was brought in to change your way, your current path, a sign to tell you that you are off-road. Get back on the road before you get lost. It is like a silent signboard telling you to change your path.

We take the illusion very seriously and assign intent and meaning to it. This creates a new illusion and takes us to a new place. This twist and turn makes us angry at life and at everyone else. It never occurred to us that all this time, we are creating this but blaming everyone else.

Don't blame yourself, for you are not really aware of what you are creating. You are not even aware of your creative ability and you do not know that you have this ability. You are not aware of this because you have not connected all your three aspects; your body, your mind, and your soul. The connection will tell you what's happening. Only the body-mind duo is at play. Your soul is not in play. So it's time to wake up.

I agree. We have kept our soul on the bench and in the booth too long. Without our soul, we are unable to see through illusions. When we bring the soul off of the bench and into the play, we will know and see the illusion and walk right past it. The illusion will vanish. Recognizing the illusion is not a skill; it's just an understanding we need to apply. It's always there; it's a part of you not yet awakened. Like Rip Van Winkle, it's been sleeping for a long time—many years. It is time to awaken.

Don't let the illusion overtake you. It's not meant to; however, it could if you allow it to. This is the choice you face every day, to engage or not to engage. When you engage and activate all three aspects of your being, you will see the illusion. This will allow you to wake up and move through life the way it was always meant to be. In fact, it will guide you through with a smile on your face saying, "Ha! I know this because I know myself better than what the illusion is trying to show me. I don't need the illusion anymore. I remember and I am remembering now." At this time, you will become truly enlightened. Light from your dark tunnel will flood in, making you remember, and enlightening your three aspects to become one blinding light for everyone to see and for everyone to know.

Ancient scriptures tell us we are built in the likeness of God, yes, in the very essence. That is our smart core in the post-physical stage. Why not keep it in our physical stage too?

There is no difference in the post-physical stage and in the physical stage, because, in the body form, you become fearful, just the way a child feels on his/her first day when he/she goes to school—from a place of comfort to an unknown place. At this point, fear walks in and guides you because clinging to fear allows you to keep the thought of your loving home intact and in focus. The child is worried that he/she may forget their loving home as he/she walks into school, and uses fear as the bridge to stay connected. As a child, you are not sure that by evening, your parents will return to take you into their arms and into their loving home. The absence of love allows fear to walk in. This cannot happen if you know you are love and the situation in front of you is an illusion to help you remember. Your ancient books tell you, "Fear not, I am with you always." What is meant here is that your soul is always with you so you are never alone, and so, never fear—just reach out.

This makes fear our non-playing character, our NPC. We need it because it keeps us hopeful. Fear creeps in and stays with us as accompanying baggage because fear is the opposite of love, and when love temporarily vanishes, fear bridges the gap. We have unknowingly created our first illusion and our many several to follow. In true reality, nothing has changed; the loving environment of the child's home moved in time and place to the kindergarten class where the child continues to be loved but does not recognize this. Children do not know that besides their parents, others can love them too. The child rejects this and waits for the only love he/she knows. In doing so, the child has created his/her first illusion. Going forward as an adult, he/she will continue to create more illusions whenever love becomes absent. Fear is our substitute teacher, appearing to make you stay focused on the love you knew when you left home.

This is exactly what happens when you separate at birth to be born as a human. Suddenly, you left your loving place where there was nothing but love and came to this earth as an infant. The place you knew as love is no longer with you, just like the child who goes to school every day from his/her loving home. You start to embrace fear; this is natural. But you need to let go as you grow up with the help of your soul. Love is all there is—fear comes in only when love is absent. Without fear, you would never know the intensity of love. Here is your exact opposite brought in to teach you about love, not a classroom lecture, but a real-life experience, a knowing by feelings. Now if you make fear your best friend, your illusion will deepen and you will skip the experience of loving and being loved. Fear is only a bridge to walk through; it's not your boardwalk. Use fear as the staircase to get to the next level. Don't stay long in the staircase or take too long to climb it. Never be confused about these two concepts; you have to experience both in life to understand both clearly. The two opposites have come together to show you what love is as known in the absence of it, and fear is the derivative that appears temporarily when love does a no-show. This is in our physical state; in our post-physical state, fear has no place because we know that we are love and we do not need another to show, tell, or convince. In our post-physical state, we are fully aware of this all the time.

So the question is why don't we remember this in our physical state?

Because physicality is all about experiencing it, feeling the fear and the love and getting to know that while fear is transitional, a bridge and a staircase, love is all there is. There is no need to cling to fear; it is an illusion, a teacher, trying to teach you about love. As we all know, FEAR is an acronym for False Evidence Appearing Real. This is the real meaning of fear. This is one of the many illusions that appear to all of you as a contextual field for you to know, embrace, and engage with love. Here is how an illusion is created by all of you. Your perspective of any situation creates your perception, your perception creates your belief, your belief creates your behavior, and your behavior creates your experience. So you can start with a perspective on anything and create an illusionary experience and stay in it long enough for you to make it your reality. Ask yourself, "What if my perspective is totally inconsistent with the actual reality?" Then see how far you are in the opposite direction. When in doubt of any perspective, ask your soul. Tell your mind to go out of the body. In the soul, the true reality will show itself to you and then, your experience will be so totally different. The illusion vanishes and true reality appears. You are a magician and a creator. You can either create an illusion or create a reality. In this, all of you have free will. What will you choose now? The universe is waiting and watching.

Choose Wisely

Chapter 7
Unify All Three Aspects of Your Being

We now know that all human beings were created in three parts or three aspects; a body, a mind, and a soul.

Yes, let's see how this works. Look at this configuration as you see a computer. All computers come with hardware, software, and an energy component. The idea and the design of the computer originally came from the way you are constructed as a human being. The only difference between you and the computer is an additional element: consciousness. Today, computer manufacturers are trying to add Artificial Intelligence programs to computers to make the machine respond and act like a human being, substituting consciousness with machine intelligence. What they are trying to do is replicate the human being in a machine form, hence the term "machine intelligence." While AI is growing in leaps and bounds, human consciousness is not keeping pace. That is why people talk about the risk of machines taking over humans. Unless your consciousness grows in leaps and bounds, creating machine intelligence does not serve your purpose. This will slow down your personal evolution and, in turn, lead to slowing down of collective evolution. At this point, machine intelligence would have overtaken human development, so the threat is real and possible unless all of you take a quantum leap. No use of having advanced technology without advanced human consciousness.

So what is consciousness?

Consciousness is a state when the body, the mind, and the soul of a human being work as one unified aspect. Many people call it The Singularity. It is a unity of all the three aspects working as one aspect. At this stage, you are conscious of all three aspects in their individual structures, but you are able to apply them as one aspect. Your understanding of this creates a new level of understanding, a higher level of energy, and this is consciousness in its pure form.

So consciousness is like a runway on which we can unify all our three aspects and use it to understand, celebrate, and promote life. The runway allows the merge to happen. So blockchain technology, an emerging computer application, is a copy of this concept. The consciousness runway is present for you to run your body-mind-soul application. The runway vanishes when you stay away from using the three aspects, like a mirage on a hot desert, and re-appears when you restart using the three aspects.

This is the choice you all have. Make the runway appear or disappear. The question is what choice will each one of you take? I say, why not use all three aspects? It's the best use of given resources. Understand each aspect, unify them together to create a runway, build and develop your consciousness to live, adapt, grow, and sustain. Each aspect is pre-equipped with an inbuilt desire that has been pre-programmed like everything in this world. That's the unique signature of your creator and all of life.

What is desire in relation to this aspect?

It's a functionality that was pre-defined. All you need to do is run with it, adapt to the changes in your surroundings, and keep your life and other lives sustained.

If we apply this in life as we know, to a passenger car, let's see how this sounds. What's the desire of a car from a human point of view? To move as a unit from one place to another and carry its passengers safely?

So what can be the desire of a three-aspect human being with many smaller parts inside? To function as a human being, adapt to the given world around, evolve, sustain as a species and to remember who you really are—an individual being of a much larger Being—and experience the beauty of love, joy, and peace while interacting with all of life and with all life forms, knowing that everything is just one large connected entity, one large family of beings.

Have we done this over millions of years? Sadly no, all that we have done so far has taken us in the opposite direction. We have chosen to pursue our own individual paths to glory, fame, and name. Where have we landed? We as a species are not happy, we do not love each other and certainly, we are not peaceful. Have we chosen wisely? The blacks hate the whites, the whites do likewise, the browns are subjugated, and the yellows are indifferent to everyone else. The color of human skin has become a problem. Each color sees the other color as inferior, not realizing that this is only an external part of a great internal being. Skin color as we have seen in earlier chapters is part of the sustaining process that evolved when human beings moved from Africa to ice-covered areas that today we call Europe and America. We easily forgot that if the skin did not change color, those human beings would have perished and been unable to adapt to the cold environment and reproduce to sustain. White color was a saving grace, not a superior aspect. Black color similarly was also a saving grace, not an inferior aspect. The brown and yellow skins are just adaptations of neither too hot nor too cold surroundings.

You are all the same at the soul level, but different in the skin level today. If you focus on the skin, you can easily forget who you really are. You have given this truth your own meaning and created a superior-inferior life ladder, then built false assumptions on the rails of this ladder. Here you are today with all of these false notions, which are just illusions. You are using these illusions to gain an advantage over one another, to enrich yourself over another. The simple truth is you are all the same in the core of your beings. The illusion has grown so large that it separates you today. Have you chosen wisely?

I agree, we have not. How can we? We barely understand this after millions of years surviving in a basic form. As we come across multiple situations from birth until death, we unknowingly inject new meaning. Each new meaning and situation makes us choose what we do, the actions we take, the words we speak and the deeds we do. This creates illusions, and in this, we make our home and over time, we believe it. This is the way we live now, hardened with belief systems created from illusions.

If you do this all the time to profit yourselves only, you end up creating a fracture in your three aspects. A fracture, as you all know, starts as a crack, and rapidly develops into a broken part. A broken part then no longer becomes functional. What is not functional cannot serve you well. A rift forms in your unified three aspects and you start to live in one aspect—your body. Since your mind is programmed to protect your body, your mind adds layers of ego to build a protective layer to sustain this aspect. The third aspect, your soul, is left out in this power play. It is forgotten and stays silent as this drama plays out. Leaving the soul out of this play makes you increase the degree of separation. Without the soul, you are all different. It's the soul that can help keep you unified.

I can now see what we have done all these millions of years, we have chosen to separate and increase our separation aspects by choosing to judge human beings on external aspects—color, height, build, form, knowledge, wealth, material possessions, and so on. We have chosen over millions of years to create millions of separation aspects as we progressed, thereby building a large reservoir of human traits that makes somebody better than the other. We never saw the opportunity to unite, because we forgot the one part we all have—the soul, the common element and the most gifted part of our being.

This understanding is true, so what are you doing with this new knowledge? Is this going to stay as knowledge or are you going to convert this to wisdom by applying this knowledge to change your life? You know that wisdom is knowledge applied and experienced. To apply it is to experience it. When experienced, your understanding of what you experienced becomes new knowledge. This grows, and over time, your consciousness starts to build and develop. This is mastery, your first step to growing into HEBs—highly evolved beings.

While we want to, it's a huge job to make everyone think this way. The survival instinct kicks in, and then fear, anger, and such other emotions add to the bias we have about color, form, shape, and language. All of this begins to interfere with our thinking. Feelings are something we struggle with. Until we get comfortable with feelings, I am afraid we will all be stuck in our old ways.

Your thought processes are affected by external factors, so judging another comes easily. All of you have extremes of emotion. Emotion is your liability. Fear and anger are leading examples. Anger in a human being reflects many biochemical changes within your metabolism. When you are threatened, fear and anger increase your reflexes and to some degree, your strength. This illusion makes you feel powerful. This was programmed to protect and defend your life, not to use it as aggression on another life form. Don't be fooled by the illusion of a sudden surge in strength. Use it wisely to defend and sustain life, not to take another life. Again, the illusion appears as a teacher to tell you the truth. Drop this illusion to understand reality. The surge in strength is a defensive mechanism to protect your life, not take another life. Once again, you allowed the illusion to become your reality, because you refused to consult your soul.

I agree; we are reactionary beings. This eliminates higher thought processes, reducing us to creatures of instinct, a useful survival trait for our more primitive ancestors to evolve. Today, we are unlikely to be chased by a saber-toothed tiger, so it's time to get rid of the survival instinct. We do not need to fear anymore. It's time to overcome these emotions as we prepare for our next stage in evolution. I am now aware that the only language our soul knows is feeling. While we can visually see color, form, shape, and hear and understand a language, we lose sight of what our soul is trying to say through feelings. It is simply trying to guide us through the valley of love, joy, and peace. We can't feel it because we are so busy doing what our mind has set in motion to make our bodies happy. While it is easy to use our visual and cognitive ability to recognize, evaluate, and judge physical attributes, we have not yet developed our non-physical ability to tune into our feelings. We didn't have to. Life gave us plenty of toys to play with. Acquiring these toys, and then retaining them and using them took all of our time. By the end of it, we grew old and then we died with fear, anger, and bias still retained inside us.

In the life you live on earth, there is no incentive to learn and understand true feelings. This is the language of the soul. You can create machine and computer languages, but you do not have time to learn your own soul's language. See how far you have gone from your most core aspect. This book would not have been possible if you were not able to tune in to your feelings.

We can all do this too. All we need is our will to do it and our belief that bringing our soul into play is helpful, constructive, and serves our needs. This is fundamental to the process, and we need to come into this willingly, not by any form of persuasion, but by free will and collectively.

That is a point of view that needs traction power. Bringing everyone to this place is a huge development that must be done in order to go to your next level in evolution. And you don't have much time left; your planet and the environment around it is collapsing. Your creator is not concerned if you do or if you don't. You are given free will and freedom to choose. What you will choose today is the question, and the universe is waiting for the answer.

Yes, I can see that. Neither is our consciousness growing and developing nor are we protecting the place we live. It's like attaching an explosive device to our home with a timer and fighting, killing, and abusing members of our family inside the home that is wired for destruction. If your home does not explode soon enough, we will have killed each other before the explosion anyway. How intelligent is this?

Seriously, you don't have much time left, unless you hurry up.

With money floating around and everything attached to money, we are not going to wake up. It's time to call for help. Money has driven skill development all through human history. Look at where this has taken us. We have simply refurbished our caves with material luxury, upgraded them to five-star caves. Millions of years later, where are we? True, we are more comfortable than before. Our living standards have evolved, our ways of life have rapidly changed, but our minds are nearly at the cave level. Survival, competition, possession are still at prehistoric levels. The only differences today are the items in play. What has changed are hunting tools, cave space, fire, fur, and so on. Primitive needs have been replaced by current needs: house, car, money, credit card, job, power, and so on. What changed were the items, not the real nature of the needs. In the past, cavemen fought over their basic needs. Today, we fight over our needs too, maybe not with stone tools or cudgels but with weapons of significant force. Is developing sophisticated weapons an achievement? Or is it simply a need to protect our possessions? In real and true terms, nothing has changed—the need to own, the need to protect our possessions has remained constant over millions of years. Is this truly an advancement?

While you evolved physically, you have mentally stayed at prehistoric levels, or near about. Money changed everything. The introduction of money brought into human society collateral issues. The need to get more, to have more, and to keep having more and more began to develop. Life started to revolve around money. This only benefits your body and puts your mind to work with the body. Your soul stays forgotten. Can you now see where this is leading? Too many body pleasing experiences dull your powerful mind and addicts you to this way forever. Your mind is now tuned to bring you more and more of bodily pleasures, and you need more and more money to keep this going. This vicious cycle continues in a never-ending loop.

I can see now how our mind and our body are addicted to pleasures and no longer available for human development. Our soul silently watches these unfolding events with sadness and aloofness and resigns to the inevitable— nothing to expect and nothing to look forward to. Our mind is very loyal to the body and follows our pleasure trail. Just like Netflix follows your movie choices and brings up more titles to please you, so does the mind follow your physical choices and lead you to more of the same. The picture now starts to get clear; we are creating what we want, not what we need. And our soul is totally forgotten. So what is our soul? Let's go back to our computer analogy—hardware, software, and the energy to power on and make both the hardware and software come alive.

Without an energy source, both the hardware and software of a computer are useless. In this very same way, without your soul, your body and mind are useless. It's what we call death, a state where your soul leaves you and your body disintegrates. The soul has no reason to stay. It's too much of a body experience, too much of it. Have you not noticed how one of your friends walks away when you neglect him or her? Just like that, the neglected soul also goes away, and you go into another state of being. So if all of your life you skip, avoid, and pretend not to understand your soul, what do you think happens? It starts to feel lonely, disconnected and slowly starts to delink from you. Disease, damage, depression, and death are consequences of too much mind-body collaboration and not enough soul connection. Disease, damage, depression, and death can be minimized and eradicated when all three aspects of our human being are connected to function as one unified part. This is the only truth there is. As you are told, the truth will set you free. When your body becomes non-habitable for the soul and the mind, both have to leave, no choice. Your body becomes uninhabitable because your cells are not reproducing enough or multiplying at a very high level. How can the soul and the mind, two metaphysical aspects, continue to live in a dying physical body? However much you want to, it's not natural. An exit is imminent.

So you are saying, without our soul, the energy source, we can't survive? It's the end of all physicality?

Technically yes. Your soul never makes this choice. You do, in your body-mind format. You shut the doors for your soul. You can live a full life. The energy source is with you by choice and will stay with you. Not using it is your choice. It's like asking if an energy source will always be available for you to use your computer or such devices. As long as electricity as an energy source is made available, yes, you can. Will electricity be shut down? Probably never for more than a short power outage, so why should your energy source be shut down?

But we have a choice to make and it's freely available all through our life to develop all three aspects of our being. We are free to develop and equally free not to do so. This is the choice we are given. We can be creators or we can be separators. Limiting our creation or expanding it is a choice we are given. Fulfilling our body desires does not last; our body is matter and form. All matter and form eventually must expire. Why are we quickening this process by choosing to stay in the body mode?

All organic forms expire at some time. You may be organic in form, but you have two non-organic support systems. Your mind and your soul are non-organic. Using these two aspects, you are able to prolong your organic life. Your ancient ancestors each lived for hundreds of years. Some lived to 400 years. Your body is fully capable of this lifespan, but only if you seek the support of the two non-organic aspects you all have. So what are you waiting for? It has become difficult for you to abandon your ways of life which your body has grown accustomed to, supported strongly by your mind that has developed to support your body. This circular logic will never end unless you want it to.

I agree; everything we do today is supporting our body need. Our mind supports the body and all its needs every time, even when it's not good for us to do it.

That's how your mind is designed. It protects your body; that's its prime objective. Your body is the weakest out of the three aspects and needs protection. But when you bring the soul into play, it works with your mind to moderate your body desires and bring in balance. This can happen only when you call for it and need the soul to come into play. You have free will and this will never be imposed on you. Until this happens, the mind will try and fulfill what the body wants. It is a powerful executor, until such time as the soul is brought in.

To keep this body drama going, we need money. To get money, the giver of money says you need to do this and we do it. I can see how this vicious cycle keeps us going. Doing it the other way, our soul tells us. You have everything you need, just give to another.

As you keep giving, you start getting the same to allow you to give more to others. Now you don't need money anymore, because what you are giving is causing you to have abundantly more of what you gave away. And this is making you happy, making you stay loving, and a peaceful feeling starts to develop and engulf you. When all three aspects are working perfectly, depression, disease, damage, and death are no longer an issue. The two non-organic aspects and one organic aspect have found unity. The alchemy of life is working to serve you.

By doing so, we are no longer addicted to pleasing our bodies alone. We have included our other two aspects. This is inclusion in the best form. If we are unable to practice inclusion in our three aspects, how will we do it with other human beings, how will we practice it in the world we live in, in the place we work in, in the home we live in? Inclusion starts with us, from within us. Developing our self is not selfish; it is the starting point to become selfless. What can you give others that you do not have? We have a choice and free will. It's better to think and choose wisely.

Yes, from a small you, become a larger you; from an individual you, become a collective you; from a local you, become a universal you. This is choosing wisely from the resources you have. Look not at what the earth has to offer you. Look at what you have to give to this earth, your home. Make this earth a nice place not only for you but for all of you to live in love, in joy and in peace. It is said in your ancient scriptures, "Go forth and multiply." Yes, you did that. It's time to switch this up one notch. Let's include our soul and make it a threesome party. In your language, one is boring, two is company, and three is a party, so bring it on. Choose wisely.

To summarize, let's change from a transactional way of life to a relational way, by forming a community of our body, mind, and soul and then stay collective, as we continue to evolve.

Language

Chapter 8
Use Feelings Instead of Words to Communicate Universally

This is one of my favorite subjects for discussion. Long ago, many hundred thousand years ago, human beings communicated in grunts and signs. Someone would point at a deer, grunt, and mimic throwing a spear. That's all it would take for others to understand. We have come a long way from this point. From a grunt and a mimic to speech, text, words, pitch, tone, and intonation, it's been a very long journey. Although we still grunt, a carry forward of our ancient ancestors' way of life, today we have 6,900 different languages. A grunt and a mimic at that time was a universal language uniting all of humanity. The 6,900 languages we have today are dividing humanity. This division is not in our best interest and is anti-evolution. Johanna Nichols—a linguist at the University of California, Berkeley seems to have argued in 1998 that vocal languages must have started diversifying in our species at least 100,000 years ago. In the words of Q. D. Atkinson, a professor from the University of Auckland, New Zealand, "Successive population bottlenecks occurred in our African ancestors who migrated to other areas, leading to a decrease in genetic and phenotypic diversity. It can be argued that these bottlenecks also affected culture and language, suggesting that the further away a particular language is from Africa, the fewer phonemes it contains." Atkinson also suggests that language first evolved around 350,000 to 150,000 years ago, which is around the time when modern Homo sapiens evolved.

Out of all the separation ideology components, this is the most decisive aspect; this is separation in its true form. Language and words are the most inefficient mode of communication because they can easily be manipulated to suit the agenda and purpose of the speaker, deceiving the listener. Language is also the Great Barrier Reef of humans, the champion of the separation ideology and the tallest among the divide and live tribe. Language and words are nothing but a manipulative human way of telling someone what you really don't want to tell. It's a clever mutation of true feelings, more on the inefficient side. Feelings, on the other hand, are more direct, clear, transparent, and truthful. This is the language of your soul; right now, I am speaking with you through these feelings. Because they are pure, you are able to understand. You only need to look at your writing to see the clarity.

Yes, I can see that, but as a human being, I am not able to speak to another via feelings.

True, but if you can sponsor your thoughts with true feelings, regardless of the language you use, the result and the effect can be way better than how you communicate today. You will be surprised at the peaceful way your communication will flow out. When everyone does this, your world will change; it will become a paradise on earth in your language.

Absolutely, no doubt about it and we need to work towards this. The most extensive catalog of the world's languages, generally taken to be as authoritative as any, is that of Ethnologue, published by SIL International, whose detailed classified list as of 2009 included 6,909 distinct languages. If this number is divided among the global population, roughly every 800,000 people speak a different language, different words that have different meanings, live in a different culture, with a different history and origin. There are 6,909 different kinds of people out there. Do we stand a chance to unite this vast number? It's a task that is not only daunting but nearly impossible. How did we come to this point?

You allowed it to happen because, in your core, you think you are different, you love to be different, and this gives you the individuality you seek. Just the opposite should have evolved—one language with multiple accents. Individuality cannot stand as it has always. The human race must get collective. Trust will solve this separation. Finally, you will be able to love your neighbor as written in your ancient books.

It's a huge task to get 6,909 languages to merge into one language. It appears to be mission double impossible unless we come out with something similar to the concept of cryptocurrency. Although the similarity is vague, we can compare it to the concept of having one electronic currency used all over the world rather than the hundreds of individual currencies we have today, each so complicated that the exchange rate for each creates huge problems for everyone dealing with it. In one brush stroke, cryptocurrency took away this complication. For everyone, suddenly one form of currency became available. The use of cryptocurrency may be questionable due to hidden and illegal purchases done on the dark web, but this is a human issue. The concept is solid. We need to come up with a crypto language that can be used by everyone. Goodbye 6,909 languages.

Although you were all created similar, you grew up differently. Every religion told you to unite. Despite all this, you chose a different path, and you wanted to be truly different. This want manifested into all the languages you speak today. This is separation ideology working overtime to divide and subdivide your species in unrecognizable ways. Do you have a chance to unify all of these people into one common platform? Yes. Start by understanding your feelings. Allow your soul to collaborate with you like you are doing right now. Tell everyone to do this. This will start a movement and a common language will emerge from this. Evolution will find a way for you, as it has over millions of years. Trust it. First, get collective—the rest will follow.

But how can we do this? This is not an off-the-shelf application we can buy and use. It's not a buy, plug and play thing. This needs all of us to remove the separation barrier between all of us. Allow the tiger, the shark, the sea snake, the octopus, the alligator, and the human to swim peacefully in the same water, metaphorically speaking. These dangerous creatures live in the sea and they are predators. We need to shed the predatory attitude as human beings living in the land. Today this predatory attitude comes out in many ways, preying on the helpless, raping innocent women, stealing from your neighbor, abducting small children, killing someone for something you want. As always, this leads to a loss of life. Life is precious. It took us millions of years for all of us to evolve. The real question to ask is how willing are we to make this stop?

You are a creator made in the likeness of your creator. You can make this happen or choose to keep it the way it is now. What will you choose, what will you do? The universe is waiting and watching. Ask for additional help from your soul. It's available, so accept it as your way forward to make you whole again, another way to be human.

Yes, it's time to seek help. We can't help ourselves anymore. We have grown so far apart, we don't see eye to eye with anyone anymore. Our bloated ego and pumped up individuality will not allow the homecoming party. We are so close to this inflection point, yet we pretend to be far away. Language and words are not relevant; they are just local adaptations by local people, from local people, for local people. We started separating years ago and perfected it along the way. Everyone knows that English or Spanish or Mandarin are not universal languages, but not knowing how to speak them can seriously harm your global interests. In all these ways, human language is so different from any other known system in the natural world that there are narrowly constrained ways in which one grammar can differ from another. For a native of Milan, the differences between the speech of that city and that of Turin may loom large, but for a visitor from Singapore, both are "Italian." Similarly, the differences we assign to grammar and sentences seem very important, but for an outside observer, it is irrelevant because he/she understands nothing. The language is just a noise, heard but not understood. As English-speaking countries developed, non-English speaking countries were left behind. All of the developments and growth in these English-speaking countries were recorded in English, never understood by a large majority, creating an economic gap and more importantly, a cultural gap. Although translation resolved this to some extent, much was lost in the translation.

Everything now divides you: culture, religion, language, and a host of several similar sub-routines. You stand divided and subdivided, and this process is only growing day by day. You have stopped using your soul to feel anymore. Today, you are so busy creating ways to differ that your soul sits in silence watching this debacle and waiting for a day when this will stop. In using your feelings, you cannot use manipulation or deceit because the soul does not employ human characteristics in the processing of feelings, simply because there is nothing new being created.

It's just remembering what it always is and was. While language is a new creation in the history of mankind, feelings are ancient. They were present millions of years ago. Simply re-member to your soul and remember, the rest will become easier.

English, Spanish, French or any such widely spoken languages gained dominance by aggression, invasion, and missionary zeal. Dominance is nothing but a slavish way of imposition. Imposing a language on a different culture and subculture of people left behind residual vapors of hostility. The language was assimilated, but the hatred remained. Dominance is not a conflict-free resolution, and such practices do not sit well for anyone.

On the other hand, engaging with feelings from your soul is a peaceful way to get everyone to participate. It is a non-violent conflict resolution. The more this happens, unity and harmony will start to flow; a powerful energy will get unleashed and this will change your world into something so beautiful, the likes of which you have never seen before.

By engaging our third aspect, our *soul*, we are only using the resource gifted to us from birth. By not engaging our soul, we only allow distorted creations to happen. Look where we all are today, just a hair's length away from total annihilation. All that we created will end when we end; however, what is created collaboratively with the soul will transcend time and live forever. The form we have today is not permanent. All forms expire sometime. As we have been told, our soul is not a form, not a matter. It is energy in vibration mode, like a halo all around us, giving us the energy to breathe and live. Imagine it to be like a space suit encasing our body but in a non-material form and shape. All human-made things have form and shape; your soul does not have shape and form;

It's time to keep aside all of the languages you learned and use your feelings to bring your understanding to the forefront. If you do this then the words that are spoken—regardless of the language used to deliver them—will become very easily understood by all. Do your basic thought construction using the mind and soul and then bring that construction to words and deeds and see the difference, the vast difference. Today, you construct your thoughts with your divided and acquired knowledge, from your ego-centered mind alone, and this leads to more division after you speak. Since your sponsoring thought is embedded in separation ideology, the outcome will also be along the path of separation in different-sounding languages. But when you use your soul, the construction of the sponsoring thought will always be kind, loving, and gentle, and so the words that come out will follow this path and the deeds that follow the words will also be soaked in these wonderful aspects. Who does not understand kindness and love when shown? You do not need a specific language or grammar or sentence construction skills to display love and kindness.

Yes, whatever language we choose to use, love and kindness will always be understood. It's a universal language. I agree that the language becomes irrelevant if the focus is on the feelings of love and kindness. Language now becomes a delivery mechanism for love and kindness to flow through. This is so different from what we do today. We do this now in just the opposite way. It is but apparent that the root cause of all divisions in this world comes from separating all of us. Language and words are a component and a high contributor to widening the separation ideology. We have nothing to be proud of; it's not important how good our mastery of the language is. What is truly important is how we can use this mastery to deliver love and kindness to all. In this context, language and word skills become meaningful because of the end result delivered. They are a medium, not the endpoint. A medium by its very definition is a path to something. If we stop at this point to perfect our language skills, then this illusion becomes real for us and we continue to stay in this illusion for as long as we want this to happen. Playing a game like Jumanji or such other games means we keep going from one level to another. Should you choose to stay and linger with a non-playing character, you get attacked. The trick is to keep moving. Similarly in life, too, don't stay too long in the illusion. Keep moving to gain higher levels of love, joy, and peace.

If you really and truly become aware that language and words are a distribution element in the process of creating love and kindness using your soul, then learning language and words becomes effective and purposeful for improving your life and those of others around you. Mastering language and words on a standalone format is what you have been doing all this time, and you have become proud of this achievement and so you are stuck in this illusion, in this bubble. Moving on will help you break away from this illusion. This can only happen if you understand language and words as elements to fulfill a higher reality. They are just a path or a tool to deliver your sponsoring thought. Giving language and words more importance than they deserve is increasing the separation ideology, not fulfilling our highest wish to express love and kindness.

And this is only possible when we engage our third aspect of our being—our *soul*. Life has a singular purpose of experiencing and expressing how beautiful we really are on the inside. The outer shell we all have is just a borrowed shell, like a tux rented for an occasion. We have to give up our shell on death to become our real self, the post-physical side of us that now is with us as our soul.

Don't look at your net worth in dollars, euros, yuan, or for that matter in any known currency. Look at your net worth in terms of love, joy, and peace that you have accumulated in your lifetime and have available to give away. This is your true net worth, which will follow you after death. All money and material things do not come with you in death; they stay behind for others to use. Your real net worth of love, joy, and peace travels with you like a mobile banking account in your post-physical stage.

That is so true, yet we want to increase our other net worth that expires on death. Somehow, we see this as our goal; in reality, it's our short-term liability. Our long-term assets are truly love, joy, and peace. Language and words are simply tools to use and to deliver the experience that we have experienced, nothing more. Reading, speaking, and writing better English, Spanish, or Mandarin may get us money and material for now, but it stops right there, nothing beyond. When we have multiple lives to lead with no money or material to accompany us from one life to another, what purpose is money and material? This makes it a short-term strategy; the real long-term resources to build up across your multiple lifetimes are the ability to think, speak, and do things lovingly, joyously, and peacefully.

This ability comes with you because it is embedded in your soul.

Given this truth, why would anyone acquire wealth other than to distribute it for all? It's not a bad or a good thing to chase after wealth and material; the sad irony is it stays behind when you die, unless you use it lovingly, joyously, and peacefully to enrich another and many others. Now that experience is worth a billion dollars, but a billion dollars will not buy you this experience. Money is of no use if it has no purpose to take you higher. Similarly, technology, religion, skin color, or any external things have no use if they do not lead you to a higher aspect of yourself. When this is done, we become complete and fulfilled.

This is the living dream manifested on earth; your life now has a purpose, your experience now has value and you have built up your net worth, ready for your post-physical stage. Your multi-life resume is now complete. You are now completed, ready to take up your next stage in evolution—

Post-Physical, aka Metaphysical as a Highly Evolved Being—HEB.

Aging, Health, and Wellness

Chapter 9
Health Is Not How
We Understand It

Age is an acronym for **A**dvanced **G**lycosylation **E**nd as per Anthony Cerami, an award-winning medical research scientist in 1980 working at the Rockefeller Foundation. Glycosylation is an important and highly regulated mechanism of secondary protein processing within cells. It plays a critical role in determining protein structure, function, and stability. When this process ends, cells are unable to reproduce, leading to the aging of a human body. The younger you are, glycosylation works well; as you get older, glycosylation advances to its end. You become feeble and bent over; muscles weaken, eyesight dims, joints stiffen—preparing you for ultimate death. King Gilgamesh, the legendary Sumerian king of the city of Uruk, in ancient Mesopotamia in 2000 BC went on a quest to achieve immortality. This is well known in ancient Mesopotamian history. Since then, all of humanity has been searching for immortality. We are looking at biology, microbiology, chemistry, and biochemistry to achieve immortality. Will we ever achieve immortality?

Your soul is immortal; your body is not. King Gilgamesh and everyone who followed thereafter did not understand this. Searching for immortality as a form is not possible. All forms and matter expire at some time. Your human body is made up of trillions of cells, chromosomes, DNA, and genes, all working in perfect harmony to keep your cells in top shape, and ultimately, your body up and running. Each cell has an inbuilt desire, a function, and a role to play. Genes are the blueprint of a cell. They control, operate, and manage reproduction for the cell.

Our scientists tell us that cellular disorders come from genetic mutation or disability in the gene. Cells need to reproduce, repair, and maintain their normal functionality. When cells reproduce rapidly, we get cancer; when cells reproduce slowly, aging sets in. The final outcome is that the cell is unable to reproduce and dies. When several of the cells begin this suicide, our body starts to deteriorate. A disease is born in the organ, where the cells are involved and where it has ceased its normal functioning. While entropy attempts to create disorder and disables this harmonious working relationship between the genes, DNA, chromosomes, and telomeres, cellular death begins and slowly leads to death. Microbiologists and biochemists are working hard to create the anti-aging gene, the first step to immortality. We want to be immortal and live forever.

Now is the time to ask why and for what do you wish to live forever? What your microbiology and biochemists are attempting to do is learn to manage disease control at best. Any advances in the study of genes and remedies only mean better disease management. While that is needed, you need to understand the root cause of your cellular malfunction. Post-malfunction is simply disease control. Each cell has an inbuilt desire to simply be what it is. When you, as a being, become unable to live in harmony with your three aspects, your desire element as a being gets disturbed. This, in turn, affects each cell's desire. This is the start of your cellular disorder, the birth of a disease, or the start of aging. Remember the network and how it is all interconnected. The cells in your body are also affected if you as a human being are affected. That's how a network works. So in reality, you are creating or rather bringing on your own problems. Because you are such a powerful creator, you can do this. You can call for this state or create joy, peace, and love or any state of mind you choose. Your cells pick up this state within you. When you exist in any one particular state, the cells in your body also mimic this state, resulting in a deviation from normal. This deviation is the leading cause of disease or early aging. In this way, you are creating your own problems by bringing on cellular disorder due to your abnormal state of being. And when you alter your state of mind, your cellular network is also altered. When you choose fear, anger, revenge, and hatred as a state of mind, it disturbs the cellular state, causing it to deviate from normal cellular function. When you choose to exist in love, joy, and peace, your cellular state returns to normalcy.

Does this mean a human being who is always in a loving, joyful, and peaceful state of mind should not expect any cellular disorder?

To a large extent, yes; however, depending on what you ingest and inject into your body, you can also change your cellular state. Cellular alteration can happen through physical or mental changes. Basically, what you feed into your body and what you feed into your mind directly affects cellular stability.

Our scientists tell us that death devours everything. It is technically an end of all of our living cells. So as I understand, death comes to all of us due to disease or due to aging. Disease is basically a cellular mutation and aging is the inability of our cells to reproduce and therefore our cells die off. With cellular death, your body also starts to age or die. Death is the end of life, another opposite to birth, the beginning of life.

Whenever you see and observe an opposite, it is an illusion, meant for you to choose or rather give you the free will to choose. Now that's true freedom! Choose life to celebrate. See through the illusion of death.

I am starting to get it now. Death—as some call it—is an acronym for **D**etach **E**nergy **A**nd **T**ransit **H**uman. If we look closely at aging and death, we can see a connection. Energy as a power source is shut down as our cells become biologically unable to reproduce. For human beings to live, our cells need to constantly repair and reproduce, and when this process slows down and ends, the human body is unable to continue living. At this point, the energy vibrations start to diminish, the body starts to age, and over time, death arrives.

It was never meant to be like this. Your bodies were designed to last for a very long time. The excessive body-mind duo enriching your body is making this happen, causing your cells to become imbalanced. This is what happens when you live in the body for too long. Health is about your internal condition, not about your external physical state. This is very important to understand. You are healthy only if all three aspects of your being are in full play—your body, your mind, and your soul. Resisting this way of life and not permitting all three aspects to come together creates cellular resistance. This resistance causes the cells to behave abnormally and starts what you call disease, and over time, aging. Molecular biology is not going to help you overcome disease and aging. At best, it can be seen as an effective disease control mechanism. Disease control is very different from having no disease at all. Molecular biology and microbiologists can only control the disease after it has occurred. You are knocking at the wrong door. Control may be a good thing, but it still is control, not an absence of disease.

That means aging, health, wellness, and death are all linked to a very critical process of use, abuse, and non-use of our three design elements or our three vital aspects—body, mind, and soul. When the body and the mind work without the soul, the cells in your body are subjected to excessive body desires. These desires, when fulfilled, work against the cell's prime desire, due to chemical imbalance affecting the cell. This imbalance causes the cell to randomly multiply or decrease cellular reproduction.

Cancer, disease, and aging follow, leading eventually to death.

You are getting the picture now. Evolution's prime directive has always been sustained reproduction of species. Sustained reproduction means sustained cellular health and wellness, giving the cell the ability to repair, monitor, and reproduce constantly. This prime directive is also embedded in your cell as a code. When humans stop reproducing, gradually the species dies off. Similarly, when cells stop reproducing, your body starts to die too. This universal and singular code is written in all of life. Life needs to create and multiply for life to evolve and sustain. This is a signature present in all living things. The reverse of this is, species vanish and individual bodies die off. All forms need to adhere to this universal principle. Seen from this point of view, aging, health, wellness, and death are abnormalities that you have brought upon yourselves, defying the natural code of life. Your human body was designed to last a very long time. It's a design so beautiful, so intricate, and so intelligent that you do not understand, and so you choose to break its fundamental code unknowingly. Know this truth and it will set you free and maybe take you down the path of immortality. Working with the body-mind duo only achieves nothing, gives you nothing, experiences nothing but a negative net worth, and more importantly does not serve your purpose.

So as I see it, working with the body, the mind, and the soul in triangulation, our bodies and our cells are capable of self-healing, if the cells are in sync with the universal song.

Our bodies and our cells have unknown self-repair potential and ability. This is possible only when the body-mind-soul are in collaboration and working as one unified part, creating the experience they were meant to create.

Instead of understanding the secrets of how your body works, how about simply unifying your three aspects and allowing your cells to do their job? They are programmed to keep you alive, healthy, young, and happy. Now immortality has a purpose. It's not your personal agenda, not your individual purpose, but a well-thought-out universal purpose. All of you are guided to this path, but who listens?

So as I can see, aging, health, wellness, and death are outcomes of not working with our three creator-given gifts. Rather, they are the result of the resistance we have put up in avoiding the use of all three aspects. Resistance always leads to trouble. At times we know, and many times we don't. What is lurking around the corner is unknown because we are not working with our full resources, not working with our extended library, not working with our unlimited knowledge of our soul. Our body is limited; our mind is also limited, meant for the limited body. So, using the unlimited soul is only adding a huge advantage to the disadvantage. And what is wrong with this, what do we have to lose? No disease, no aging, and perfect health. Aren't these worth living and fighting for? Immortality in our current stage and in our current understanding of enriching our body-mind combo will never happen, regardless of how advanced microbiology and biochemistry become. This part of the advancement will only lead to disease control getting better and better for diseases we now know. What about new diseases that come up? Microbiologists and biochemists will need to study these new diseases in the future to come up with newer disease-control approaches. We can now see the lag in the cure; disease will always come in ahead, and disease control will always lag behind. This is not a logical way to solve this problem.

You can take a new and different approach. You can start using the body-mind-soul collaboration to say goodbye to disease, goodbye to aging, and welcome to good health and a youthful body. The promise of this is so enchanting, yet so unreal that you are unable to believe in this. Immortality is not for individuals—it is for all of humanity. You will never achieve immortality on a solo basis, and it's pointless to even aspire to it. That's the way evolution is. A gift is meant for all of humanity, never for a selected few. This is the basic error in your human way of thinking. Possession of a secret for a secret few is not going to happen. That is not the way of a higher life and not the way of a higher life form. Life evolves from life and grows and sustains only if the basic rules are followed and applied. Your separation ideology is obstructing you from choosing a higher way of life.

What you mean is, as long as we stay separated—aging, bad health, and death are for sure accidents waiting to happen. We have once again got aging, health, and death all wrong, as we have with everything else this book talks about. It's time to change our conversation to really understand that not working at using our body-mind-soul combination is detrimental to our way of life, and if unchecked, will only lead to unknown dangers.

Disease control and cell control are two different things. Disease and Health are similarly two opposites. Once again, the law of opposites is in play, as always. The law of opposites is simple to understand. It is a choice for you to choose the higher aspect, a simple aid to help you choose. One is an illusion, the other is real. Nothing dangerous happens when you choose the illusion, you just get caught in it and stay in it till you decide to walk away. The law of opposites is easy to follow. Choose the higher aspect all the time and the illusion vanishes. Choose life always and you will overcome death.

So it follows the video game strategy. Engage with game characters and you progress and move ahead in the game. Engage with non-game characters and you stay stuck at the same level. This analogy is close to what I understand. The illusion is simply a reminder call to help you choose the high ground. It is nudging us to avoid choosing the low ground and staying in the illusion.

This is the way of life. You always have choices to make and ways to go. The entire universe is waiting to see what you will choose, which way you will go.

Disease is just a sign that our inner self is not happy, not aligned to the joyful cosmic song. It is a way of reminding us to change our excessive use of our bodily desires and find a more balanced body-mind-soul combination. Life extension therapies serve no purpose if they are not accompanied by the inclusion of your soul along with your body and mind. Even if life-extension therapies become successful, how would you manage the increasing number of seniors who could now live longer? This brings in a whole new conversation—what we can do to help seniors stay happy in their old age as life extends beyond what we know today. If these people were actively practicing the combined use of their body-mind-soul resources prior to reaching old age, they would be able to move through this phase with comfort—joyfully and peacefully experiencing love and expressing all of these things.

And here is the best part of our conversation. These people have the largest experience. Having lived life this long, they have seen the highs, the lows, the ups and the downs, and the good and the bad. This qualifies them to be the best child-care providers. In this way, the seniors have a path and a way to keep themselves engaged and useful to humanity while they raise another by giving them wisdom, critical thinking, and the life tools that the young need to become responsible adults. Young parents are not fully ready to parent; their inexperience makes them struggle. This struggle leads to mistakes in parental care. Why not allow seniors to raise children and impart the wisdom they have accumulated, while the young couple enjoys their youth and newly found love?

Of course, this would mean staying in a community rather than individual homes to allow collaboration and support for all seniors. No longer will old people feel lonely; rather, now they will feel wanted. This alone will remove depression and disease from their lives. Their cells will rejuvenate with energy to give them new life, and give the younger couple free time to enjoy themselves and celebrate life. Both the young and the old now stay in good health, in good condition. Goodbye disease, depression, and death for all. This is a true life extension from a higher point of view. Imagine the huge cost saving for healthcare; imagine no more mental illness and depression; imagine happy people everywhere.

Life extension by bioscience will never last if it is not accompanied by a happy life. To be healthy, you need to be happy. This is the prime ingredient. You don't need medicine or gene replacement therapy. Just be happy. This is life's wonder drug given to all of you by your creator, free of cost, free of charge, and with no obligation. Yet, you never take this simple choice but are willing to ingest and inject medical solutions, forgetting that life's most advanced cure is right within you. How ironic that you take help from everyone who only wants your money to cure you, and forget the one higher being that gives you everything with love, your soul!

Money is not a substitute for what we really need to live life. It's a human creation to create inequality, rank people and create life shelves for people to be placed, based on money, power, and fame. True life is a green pasture, filled with people smiling and living in joy and peace, free of disease, depression, and death. This is possible only if all of us work using our three aspects—body, mind, and soul.

So make that call today, dial 1-800... Soul.

Meditation
Chapter 10
Center Yourself the
Mind-Soul Merge

Wikipedia writes about meditation: "The word meditation is derived from old French meditacioun and the Latin meditatio from a verb meditari meaning 'to think, contemplate, devise, and ponder.' The use of the term *meditatio* as part of a formal, stepwise process of meditation goes back to the 12th-century monk Guigo. Apart from its historical usage, the term *meditation* was introduced as a translation for Eastern spiritual practices, referred to as dhyana in Hinduism and Buddhism and which comes from the Sanskrit root dhyai, meaning to contemplate or meditate. The term meditation in English may also refer to practices from Islamic Sufism or other traditions such as Jewish Kabbalah and Christian Hesychasm."

To center yourself simply means to align your three aspects to form a singularity in your thought, word, and deed. This is an internal process and not an external workout. External workouts can best be considered as a staging area to start meditation. However, it still is a staging area; expecting too much from an external workout may need to be managed.

This is a human way to understand meditation. True meditation is when you place yourself in a state of readiness to experience total awareness, while your body is in a wakened state. You do not need to sit down to meditate. Meditation is simply a device, a tool as you understand. In reality, meditation is nothing more than connecting with your soul. In order to connect with your soul, all of you found a way by creating a technique. The very act of doing this creates a denial that you cannot do this until you master this technique. One does not need a technique to talk to your soul, just do it. Over thousands of years, mankind has been creating one technique after the other to create a contact with your soul. What they have not been doing is accepting that you are a three-aspect being. The rest is easy. The first step in any understanding is knowing and then comes the doing. If you reverse the order, then you will never know, but you will become an expert doer. Again, this is your physicality that is showing up as it has, over thousands of years.

All of us love to learn a new technique and we feel that by doing so, we improve our understanding. Today, there is a technique for everything. Have we learned from using techniques? It works well for things like playing games, doing an activity, etc. But when you come into the world of metaphysics, doing a technique does not work. Metaphysics is not about physicality, it's just the opposite—zero physicality. We have not yet till today, understood that doing does not take you to a place of knowing. Knowing takes you to a place of doing, not the other way around. What we do not know, we cannot learn by any form of physical doing. The very act of doing creates an experience that you are trying very hard to know, which gives us the experience of trying. When you start from the core that you know and so you are doing, the experience is very different. There is no technique superior to knowing. All we need to know is that we are a three-aspect being and the third aspect is our soul and we need to make contact and stay in contact. This is mediation in its purest form.

If you can focus your mind away from a technique and to a path of knowing, then you can speak to your soul anytime you want to, then you can meditate with your eyes open or closed. It's not the physical form you assume in order to meditate, nor is it the exercise, you do to assume a physical position to meditate. You do not need to do anything, just talk to your soul. The language of your soul is feelings, just feel and sense the feeling that comes in. You don't have to leave your body to experience this. Just stop doing what you are doing, be right where you are and be in the moment. Wisdom is found wherever beauty is formed. Beauty is formed everywhere, out of all life. This is a state of complete wakefulness. In this state, you turn whatever you are doing into a meditation.

This is something we have not grasped nor understood or maybe not willing to. We have all been conditioned to think that it is by doing something that one achieves something. By placing doing ahead of knowing, we have reversed the true order of our natural state. If we want to play hockey, we need to learn. The want is the desire. All of life has desire built in, it's the universal life signature. This is your starting point. From this desire, you grow into the doing, so you learn to play hockey. It's a craft; like all crafts, it has a technique. The game of hockey or any physical activity is 100% physical, therefore the technique is important. For any physical activity, this is a must. But meditation is not a physical activity, it's a zero activity, no amount of technique will get you to the place you want to go. The more we practice our various techniques, the further we are from our destination. This is because while you are getting better and better at meditation practices and postures, you are getting weaker and weaker on the real purpose to meditate—connect with your soul, the energy you do not understand. By keeping your body still and engaging your mind to seek the energy, all we are doing is to enhance this state of being. It does not lead us to the connection we seek. True connection comes from a desire to know your soul, and therefore, doing things that make the connection possible.

Yes, this is a correct understanding, because you have not accepted your true composition—a being made up of three aspects, body-mind-soul. You have mastered the art of making your body do wonderful things by getting your mind to tell the body to do things. By not engaging your soul, you have limited yourself to your mind-body routine. You are not complete when you do not work with all three aspects. This will always limit you and so, you seek meditation techniques to get there. You cannot get to a place you do not acknowledge. While you consider your soul as something different from you, no amount of technique can get you there. Denial of this, places this far from you. What you deny, you declare. What you declare, you create. So, constantly, you are creating an experience of trying to meditate with the desire to connect with your energy. Just connect and skip the technique. By overemphasizing the technique, you have unconsciously removed yourself from the act of connection. The technique now becomes your main focus, the connection, a lower priority.

All of this book tries to tell you this very message that we do not have to do anything to get anything. We have all that we need in our soul to live and experience who and what we are. By denying this, we created artificial structures to seek the very same thing, because this makes our body important. We feel happy when we make our body important. This is necessary because we have not accepted our three aspects. Lack of the third aspect, we struggle hard to do things, hoping we can reach this state. We can all get there much faster, much quicker; all we need to do is accept and stop denying our true reality. In accepting, everything comes to you rather than you struggling to get it. Life is not a struggle, we are making it so. And we have set up techniques to overcome the struggle. There is no struggle; once we understand, accept, and live it, the struggle vanishes.

The very act to struggle establishes the fact that you do not know, hence the difficulty. It's internal resistance. Like a resistor, it will produce heat to hurt the internal parts of your body and eventually create inner conflicts. I ask you to please reverse this and tell yourself, I know, all I need to do is ask my soul. Make that conversation, make that connection, the struggle to do anything goes away, replaced with full knowing. This knowing will take you to the place you belong, to the place, you always belonged to.

Meditation is good but not effective when done through a routine or a subroutine. Anything done on a physical plain always stays on the same plain. To be able to elevate to higher consciousness, merge our mind and body to our soul. Make the threesome work together. This is true meditation. Every time we get our soul to connect with our body and mind, we are meditating. This is real meditation, moving from lower consciousness to higher consciousness by engaging our soul. Our body has nothing to do with meditation. Our minds and soul are the only players in this area. The body allows the two of our aspects to merge when we accept and desire the merger. Desire is everything, the unique life signature. When we allow our desire to merge and allow all life forms to fulfill their built-in desires, we would have created true meditation—the merging of all life to the universal oneness.

Yes, this is real meditation. By following a technique to meditate, it is very difficult to reach your goal or accomplish what you want to. A part of you is metaphysical and a part of you is physical. The two are not compatible. While you can use your metaphysical part to make your physical part do things, the reverse is not possible, rather impossible. What can work is the merger of both parts to form a fusion. Using your physical part to attain a metaphysical state is not a possible task in your current state until you reach the HEB status—Highly Evolved Being.

So what you are saying is that without unity, doing any physical activity or a technique only enhances the physical part of us. To get our metaphysical part working, we need the body-mind-soul merge. Meditation starts in a physical way and tries to take you to a metaphysical state. And you say this is not fully possible because our physicality cannot lead us to our metaphysicality unless all three aspects are unified. So now it becomes easy to meditate. Know and accept our three aspects and collaborate with all three aspects to generate an experience. This will lead us to everyday meditation, done with ease, done with full knowing and without the rigor and the rigid postures and positions we have to assume to go into meditation. The word meditate now changes its metrics and visuals completely from what we know to what we do not know. All of this cannot be done by external instruction or coaching. This has to come from within you, the knowing and accepting.

Do not give up what you are trying to do. It's an honest attempt towards moving to a desire. So while you continue on this path, be mindful that an exercise, a technique, a workout are best for the body. Your mind and your soul needs no exercise. It only needs a connection to your body, hotwire it and see how your internal engine roars to life and takes you to places you never knew possible. So meditate all you want, but with the body, mind, and soul connected.

People have meditated for years and never experienced the connection. Daily meditation is a good thing. It requires your commitment to seek inner experience, not outward reward. The sound of silence is the song of your soul. Believe in the silence of your soul, rather than the noises of this world. All of life is meditation. Walk in wakefulness. Move with mindfulness, not mindlessly.

Bringing It All Together
Chapter 11
The Final Roll Out

The truth is so deep yet so simple that we skip it, to stay shallow, for this path is an easy path to take. We look for instruction, pretending we don't have any. We forget that we have a GPS in our *soul* to take us where we should be going. This is the deep truth, waiting for you to embrace it willingly. Color, separation, possession, villain, victim, illusion, form, money, language and words, and aging and health are all aspects of human-created separation ideology and pure human concepts. They do not exist anywhere else except on earth.

In reality, these are parts of a conceptual canvas manifested to allow you to reject all of these aspects of a human being because you are none of this. To merge into each of these illusions is easy, it's like jumping into a flowing river and swimming with the current—much less effort. That's not the place you want to be. Just because the river is flowing, there is no need to dive in. The river exists for life forms in the water to exist and is a human resource. That's its function and purpose. Diving into the river of illusion alters your main purpose. Function, purpose, and desire are found in all of life. All you need to do is observe, learn, and apply.

I understand we have free will to do so. This does not mean we chose to do so. We can choose to or we can choose not to. This is the option we all have. What will we choose as a species, where will we go with our selection? Over the millions of years we have wandered on this earth, we have not yet determined our purpose. What we see today in this world is living proof that we have not chosen wisely so far.

All of life bears a universal signature. It is all connected, a vast network of interconnected living things. Wherever you see interconnected things, you can be sure it's all one big thing divided into many smaller parts to allow every form of life to exist and support one another. When the design is interconnected, why are you separating and fracturing every part of this network?

This detaches us from the network. We need to stay attached. This is the true purpose of all life, to stay attached and build the local network around your area. As each local network station begins to create and develop, other networks benefit and grow. We all grow together. The network starts to strengthen. In our world today, we have the World Wide Web. We are all connected on the net digitally, but on the ground, we stay fractured as smaller family units. The digital connection is giving us clues to get together, yet we choose to avoid this blatantly because we want our smaller family unit to get all it can, even if our larger family does not. This is the opposite of a network characteristic. This is breaking up the network for our smaller needs.

Networks survive when they stay connected and grow, and are allowed to consume universal resources placed at the disposal of the network. Your Earth was given abundant resources, and a primary network was established. Air, water, and food, the three basic elements of life were given to you wherever you lived. All other resources were distributed around the four corners of the earth in the hope that each of you living in that corner would share with others in the other corners, like a large family bringing something from their individual homes to a family home get-together. If you can do this within a household, why is it so hard to do this outside the household with the larger human family?

We parceled ourselves into separate kingdoms and then into nations and then into communities and then into genders and finally into belief systems. We can clearly see the separation construction at work. This separation is developing and growing. The network is broken. Smaller groups of humans live and protect their resources, while others live without any resources. Sharing was replaced by greed; distribution was replaced by acquisition and storage. Finally, living together was replaced by me and my family only. We are getting very good at separating everything we were given. How is this any form of intelligence? How is this any form of higher evolution? To keep is easy; to share is the hardest part. Yet, over millions of years, we were assisted by multiple forms of messaging to abandon our current way of life and accept a unified way of life. Every religion tells us to share, look after the poor, and help the needy. Who listens? Who is listening? Every religion on this earth also tells us to stay together; every family tells each member to stay connected. Yet, we choose not to universalize this concept to take it outside our family home.

The world you live in today is completely fractured. You are detached from the original design of a large powerful network. This detachment is hurting all of you and bringing misery, disease, depression, and finally death into your world, far too early and too rapidly. It does not have to be this way. All of you can change this by working with your soul more actively.

Yes, it's time we did this. Today, we know that death is **D**etach **E**nergy **A**nd **T**ransit **H**uman, where our soul leaves us to go away. This is a state where we no longer exist as a body, a state brought upon by our choice because we did not stay within the design parameters. It's a universal creation concept. All manufactured products expire long before their expected life cycle because of incorrect usage, abusive usage, or faulty workmanship. Our human life follows this very path. The only difference is that the human body is a perfect creation and is capable of sustaining a high degree of abuse, unlike a manufactured product that is imperfect on a comparative basis. The human body is perfect. We make it imperfect by our way of life. It is not possible, at least not now, to create a more perfect thing or an object or a form or matter better than a human body: millions of cells working together as a network to sustain the body in its original specifications. What we have done in our lives is the opposite of this wonderful creation. We have successfully partitioned our mind, body, and soul to separate from the original design, unplugged ourselves from the vast network we were given, only because we wanted more of it to ourselves, to our smaller family, to our smaller thought and belief system. We abused resources on earth and we call ourselves developed beings. Our Earth is losing its inbuilt resource network because we are consuming too much of it in some parts and leaving other parts without any of it. We are living in the opposite way of our original construction and design.

It's like living in a house, chipping away at its walls, floors, roof, and structures because you want everything for your smaller room at the back, where your family lives. You really don't care if others lose their rooms and have nowhere to go. You are proud of doing this because self-enrichment is what you seek, not enrichment for all. Your narrow ways of life, your smaller way of thinking, your restricted views of this beautiful earth, abundant with richness, only to keep it for your smaller purpose is what is causing everything to happen that is happening today. You are unplugged. You are unhinged from creation. It's your belief system and your way of thinking that is causing all of this to happen. Change this and you will change the world you live in. If you can't do this alone, seek help that is available from your soul.

When we forget our prime purpose of life, we tend to make our own purpose, a smaller narrow version of the original purpose. A divided purpose never serves everybody, because the word "divide" is the starting point of separation. Divide to unite later is a conscious way of understanding life. Then, divide becomes an action understood, not a re-action misunderstood. Unite is the keyword here; divide is the starting point, not the continuing point. The continuing part is the illusion we have embraced. The start and endpoints are reality; the middle portions are illusions. If we all remember that we divided to unite, we can easily play the illusion: look at your playbook and make your moves. Look right at it and do not be affected by it. Instead, use it to stay on course.

When your three-year-old goes to school every morning, he or she walks out of his or her home and into a different place you call school. Is this separation? It's a temporary absence for sure. When school is over, your three-year-old returns home to be united with his or her family. Let's take this concept and stretch it a lot wider. You are born, you walk away from your creator, you die, and you unite with your creator. For the time you are away, it may not be school time for you, but it is definitely off time. What you do with this time is your free will. What will you do, pretend you are someone else and forget your true origin? This is the illusion created to help you live on earth as a human being, but with a purpose to express and experience who you really are. The illusion is meant to help you get there. It's not meant for you to stay and embrace the illusion; rather, use it to advance to your true destination. When you all do this, take the starting point—birth—and the endpoint—death—as a process you will enable your experience and expression to manifest. This earth will become a wonderful place, a true paradise, a heaven, a place to live and prosper, in your language, because you now remember who all of you are. And when you do, all separation will end.

When an artist copies an idea from another painting, the painting becomes a reproduction. When the artist creates a painting from ideas generated from within, an original is created. The former is a reaction and the latter is a creation. When we deal with life with our mind and body, it's nothing but a reaction, because the mind is only capable of storing past experiences. So we tackle a situation today with the experience of yesterday—nothing but a reaction. When we tackle a situation today in a new way, a way given to us by the combination of our mind and soul working together with our body, we will be creating, not reacting. Creation will lead us to a better way to deal with the situation at hand. Reaction will only cause the same effects that happened before, with some minor changes. When we come into the situation armed with the knowledge of who we really are, we control the situation; the situation does not control us. We stay in charge; the situation is not playing us. When we stay in control, we can shape the situation and take it to its intended resolution, conflict-free, violence-free, shaped by the mind and soul working in unity with the body to create the next highest thing. This is another way to be human. If separation is what we are currently practicing, then what are some unification factors?

Yes, another way to be human: the exact opposites—patience, compassion, kindness, mercy, joy, peace, and love. When you apply these to any situation at hand, you are creating from your true self, not reacting from your acquired self. These unifying factors help creation and stop reaction. Regardless of how ugly the situation is, working from your mind only does not help. Using your mind and soul can help uplift the situation, challenging you.

So you are saying, from our mental toolbox, let's take out our kindness screwdriver, our compassionate hammer, and our happy screws. Use these tools for every situation we come across and keep working this until it becomes a habit and the only way we know. Our tool kit is not physical; it is *metaphysical*. Don't look for the steel screwdriver, or the cast-iron hammer, or the alloy screws. Let's use our mind-soul duo to create the same effect of using a physical tool.

In the early origins of human beings, grunt, noise, tools, and later on, speech and text formed to shape your communities. This shut off mental development and started physical development. This is why, even today, you are well-developed in using speech and tools, but under-developed in understanding metaphysical concepts. Your early origins never moved you along this path. This can change starting now. Without any need for the survival instinct, you can begin developing your metaphysical understanding.

In my understanding, it's about time we did this. Time to get away from mass and muscle and dive into metaphysical concepts.

A happy person, a compassionate person, a peaceful person, and a loving person is what you are, what you have always been before birth and will be after death, so why forget this while living? The illusion may have caused you a temporary memory lapse because the illusion is meant to do this. As you live in this created illusion, your higher awareness should wake you up and allow you to create while the illusion is still running circles around you. So wake up from all of the illusions you took yourself into.

Let me create an analogy. Imagine we are standing in a room with a high ceiling and with windows only near the high ceiling. Suddenly the room starts to flood and the water starts to rise. Our instinct tells us to swim and try to reach the high ceiling to open the window and get out. This comes to us naturally. We don't need to receive any instruction. The rising water in real life is the illusion. Rise out of it by opening the window of your higher being, your higher aspect—love, peace, and joy—and the illusion will vanish, the water will recede, because we have now remembered to apply what we have always been—a being of love, existing peacefully in a joyous state for all of eternity.

Yes, that is a good analogy. In this earth, as human beings, you have forgotten this metaphysical DNA and you focus on your physical body DNA. Your soul has no separation aspects. This is why the exact opposite is

brought into existence on earth for all of you, to understand
and remember that following the illusion is not your way.
Using the illusion to rise above and create is your only way.
Creation has no limits; it is unlimited. When you reach the
highest point in the way you understand, your energy levels
will expand to allow a higher level of understanding to
come into existence. This goes on because your creator is
also unlimited and expanding in every way.

So true, we have a long way to go. A large capacity is
sitting idle at this moment, waiting to be used. Do not be
fooled by our current physical brain capacity. As we grow
in our creative ability, additional meta-capacity will come
our way. It will not come to me or to you as individuals. It
will only come to us as a collective, for all of us. This is
why all of us have to be unified to receive this higher gift.
Separating each of us is not helping to get this additional
capacity. All of humankind gets this higher power, or none
of us get it, so stop chasing individual pipe dreams and get
everyone on board. There cannot be one superman or one
superwoman. All of humanity needs to become a
superspecies.

Yes, don't aspire to create superhuman beings. Aspire
to create a superhuman species. Include all of it to become
all of it. Don't look at color, separation, possession, villain,
victim, illusion, and such complementary concepts as ideas
to absorb and promote in your human life on earth. It's time
to shed these concepts and embrace your true self, a pure
being of love, peace, and joy, living in harmony with all of
life, dealing compassionately with every situation and with

*every incident, now and all the time. All of life is valuable. All of life is precious. It's a gift given to you to cherish and celebrate. It's your prime responsibility to protect, sustain, and promote all life without labeling, segregating, classifying, and without separating. For you were all **one**, before. You do not remember. It's time to re-member.*

This is the hard part to remember. To re-member is much further away. Merriam Webster dictionary defines symbiosis as "The living together in more or less intimate association or close union of two dissimilar organisms." We must try and make our soul our symbiotic partner to our minds. Our minds and our soul are two dissimilar aspects of our human being. The close union of these two aspects is to our best and highest advantage. Evolution is waiting for us to choose this way of life. We may not see it this way today, but this is the only way, the only path to becoming a higher being. Allow evolution to run its path, and it will take us to higher ground. Get out of its way by standing out of its way. Life is too large to stay restricted, to stay handcuffed to thinking that arises from survival instincts. Survival is no longer relevant. There are no more saber-toothed tigers chasing us. Separation is a close cousin to survival. As long as we harbor the survival instinct, separation instincts will get stronger inside us.

*It's time to shed your survival instinct. I say it's high time to do this. Do not be confused with memory, awareness, and consciousness. **Memory** is physical, a storage area in your mind of all the things you've done and acquired in your past. Awareness is not memory. **Awareness** is when you* *work using your mind and soul as a duo, allowing your mind to use the library of the soul rather than the memory of your mind. When you do this and you continue to do this and this becomes your way of life, you will become conscious of the fact that your mind and your soul are now working together to raise you to higher **consciousness**. With higher consciousness, your energy vibration will increase, giving you more energy, higher intelligence, and a higher way of life. At this point, you will realize that separation and other things we talked about in this book are irrelevant. The only things that matter are universality, loving and respecting all of life, every part, every big and small part, because all of life is one unified aspect, with a desire to experience and express.*

We can only attain this level when we work with our soul, not with our mind as the solo player. So, are you ready to take on this new role?

Evolution always starts at a physical level when the species is young, to allow the physical body to adopt and adapt to the natural environment with a prime directive of reproducing and multiplying. This feature is strongly protected at all times. This process takes thousands of years, and once the body and the environment become adaptable with reproduction at full capacity, evolution then moves on to take a social aspect to bring a community in to focus— social evolution. This means large numbers of people staying together, helping each other to develop and evolve. This is the starting point for the large human social network. At the basic core of this network is the single-family unit, with two parents and children. This basic unit then lives in a community, several communities form a region, and so on. As social evolution matures, evolution then brings in science to take on a technology aspect to improve life and living conditions for all life. This technology is meant to improve living conditions for all and not for a selected few. You are stuck in this stage of life today. Technology used for gaining an advantage over others is not the reason why evolution allowed technology to come into your way of life. All of you are abusing technology to enrich yourself and not for all of humanity.

We are today using technology to dominate, kill, damage, destroy, subjugate, starve, and wipe out the basic family unit, the community, and the larger global population. We are trying to wipe out what took evolution millions of years to bring us to this point. Evolution's prime directive is being violated. Whenever the reproductive ability of a species is threatened at its basic level, evolution will find a way to reduce this threat and eliminate it. Dominance is never a part of evolution and never will be. Evolution will find a way to reduce dominance, as it has in the past.

If you can move past this stage and start to use technology for the benefit of all living beings, evolution will take you to the final stage of your human development, the metaphysical stage. Your race is now stuck at the technology level, having evolved from other levels. Technology is just a transition point, not an endpoint. You need to move ahead by using technology as a stepping point to enter your last phase—the metaphysical stage.

So you are saying at this stage, we take all of what we evolved from and convert this into post-physical aspects of all that we know so far. That is, use your mind-soul duo to do what we do as physical beings without a physical body, tools, objects, and concepts. After death is the metaphysical stage. This is our next natural stage of evolution while living.

You do not need any physical aspects to live life. It helped you so far to bring you to where you are now. It's time to switch it up, and you can't do this until all of you are ready to do it. This is the completion of your beings; this is the last stage of your development, where you learn from living in a physical way to become a metaphysical being, a hybrid of physical and metaphysical aspects. Finally, you will become a highly evolved being, embracing all of life, understanding all of life and knowing that you are all one in different forms. Color and separation will vanish to be replaced by love and bonding as one large human family. You are all brothers and sisters; all children are your children, regardless of their skin color, body shape, or language spoken. When you become metaphysical, all aspects of your body differences will vanish. You will finally have no color, no shape, no form— but you can choose any of this to become physical at any time, making color and such other factors an option and not a rank order.

So it's not a race to reach the end more quickly than someone else. It's a journey to collect everyone and bring them to this point, like a shepherd gathering his flock for the night. It's every sheep with no sheep left behind. A true shepherd does not separate his flock into good looking ones, ugly ones, fat ones, and the ones with heavy fur. He always brings his flock home together. Why can't we learn from this simple way of life, to include all life? We live the opposite way from the traditional shepherd. We reward a selected few and neglect a larger few. Competition is in the opposite direction of completion.

Complete, you will. It may take millions of years or a century or a decade or less, after disaster, disease, and death has taken its toll on humanity, or you can do a quantum jump right now into your next stage of evolution. What will you do, where will you go, and how long will you take? Humanity needs to make a decision now before evolution takes its final step. At this crossroads, you sit and wait, not knowing whether to leap or walk the same path you have always walked. It's now or never to choose your next path. Evolution is calling all of you to collect all of you and come home—to the place you belong, to the place you've always belonged.

Let's take the help and let's move on. Use all of the energy that is available to all of us and elevate and evolve to a new level. This is impossible if we hold and carry with us our currently manifested separation attitude to live in isolation. Build an elevation mechanism to elevate ourselves and others around us to become Highly Evolved Beings. This elevation is the next stage in our evolution. If we do not do this, another species will begin to appear and grow in the midst of us, assimilate us, and most probably decimate us.

Evolution sits in the middle watching and waiting for the human race to elevate itself, and should it see that this is an impossible task, it will take another approach to execute its prime directive to allow life to sustain, evolve, and develop along a safe and chosen path. Evolution will try to shift the energy of the sun to dissipate to another set of species in the hope of seeing the elevation. The Darwinian Theory of Survival of the Fittest, with a slight twist and a turn. The earth will survive. The question is which dominant species will continue to live on earth? Will you be one of them?

Unknown to us in our current stage of understanding, filled as we are with prime separation ideology components such as skin color, language, and wealth, a new set of species is slowly growing and developing and will likely take our place unless we shed our current ways of life and elevate ourselves to Highly Evolved Beings or risk our future to another species that might be willing to accept elevation as their prime purpose, with a unified sense for all, from all, and by all to experience and express the oneness of all of life—the universal energy signature of all life.

You do not have much time. Take this conversation seriously. Build on it, debate and argue, but move forward to a new way of living. It is said that you have to do a wrong thing to do the right thing. You have lived the wrong way for millions of years. It's about time to live the right way and do the right thing. Let's continue this conversation forward, keeping elevation and evolution as your prime focus and your dead center.

We have been and always will be a *being* made of love, existing in a joyful state, at peace with everything. Anything else is an illusion created for you to forget first and then remember who you really are. The process of forgetting and remembering is your experience. This is your true net worth and the only purpose of your life. Everything else is an illusion, a prop, a stage for you to play it out. Your form, your shape, your color, the language you speak, your accent or your wealth or your health do not matter. They are simply acquisitions that you gain in the process of growing up as a human. This is not what is in play. What is in play is to remember who you really are. How long will you take to remember—one lifetime or many lifetimes?

When you live as a single-aspect being, you become obsessed with matters of the body: money, power, possessions, physical stimulations and satisfactions, security, fame, financial gain. When you live as a dual-aspect being, you broaden your concerns to include matters of the mind. Companionship, creativity, stimulation of new thoughts, new ideas, new goals, personal growth, new challenges. When you live as a three-aspect being, you come into balance with yourself. Your concerns now include matters of the soul: spiritual identity, life purpose, relationship, path of evolution, spiritual growth, ultimate destiny. Evolution does not mean dropping some aspects of self in favor of others. It simply means expanding focus and turning away from exclusive involvement with one aspect towards genuine love and appreciation for all three aspects—body, mind, soul.

From an ancient couplet written many centuries ago:
We dance round in a ring and suppose,
But the secret sits in the middle and knows.

Epilogue

I urge all of you to get inspired and make that connection with your soul and start a conversation as I did. Engaging your soul as you do with your body and mind is an important journey that all of us must undertake to live life in a much better way. We are not complete without this.

This particular book and the contents herein are the conversations I had with my soul, and as a result, I reinforced my understanding of an insightful way to be human, another way to be a human. This conversation touches many subjects I shared with my soul, asking questions, arguing from my limited understanding, seeking clarity on issues and things I believed in. The response I got was amazing. The conversation uplifted me and cleared my filter and my lens to see the world in a different way. You should do the same and discover a great experience. This entire book comes from this higher conversation. It was a conversation that was going on inside me. I am now bringing it out in the open to share with all of you. It was hard, but if one tries hard enough, you too can start a conversation between a **human you** and a **soul you.**

Finally, it became so clear that I was able to engage my soul to have a spirited conversation on several subjects that shape our human way of life. It may sound very strange to many of you, but as you finish reading the book, you will notice it comes from a very high level of life. It could not have come from me alone. It came from a higher source of wisdom, my soul. A conversation that is truly a beautiful experience, an inspiration from the call to make friends with my soul was heard. This conversation is what I experienced. It's not a lecture, neither is it a judgment. It's just another way to be human, and I am happy to share this with all of you, in the hope that one day you can begin a conversation of your own with your soul on subjects that you are passionate about, and experience and express who you really are—a human being existing in three parts. Exploring all the three parts and aspects of our being is a discovery, a remarkable one that all of us must start at some time.

The first step, I say, is to accept our being as a three-aspect being—the body, the mind, and the soul. All three stay together from your birth to your death. While we engage our body and our mind, we forget our soul. This is what I am talking about in this book for all of you to accept, engage, and express willingly and freely. When you quieten your mind and shut off the external desires, demands, and doings, you will be able to see an energy surrounding your body—a vibrating energy—like a halo all around you. Start a conversation with this energy and see how you get to know it better. It's a part of you, not clearly visible as a human being but that's what a vibrating energy field looks like and this is the metaphysical part of you. The words from an ancient text now become clear, *"Be not afraid, I go before you always, follow me, I will give you rest,"* Luke 6.20. This energy field surrounding you is with you all the

159

time and rightfully so, before you. Ancient words spoken 2,000 years ago now becomes clear.

Once this sinks in, the conversation can begin and don't expect an answer right away. In time, the answer comes to you as a feeling. You will be surprised at the depth of the wisdom and the breadth of the subject matter. At this time, you will know that this is not from your human memory, or from your acquired human knowledge, or from any books you have read. It's different as if this knowledge was uploaded directly to you, just like that.

Feel the feeling, convert it into thoughts, and put these thoughts to work as words, written or spoken, and then take action in what you do and say. As you go about this, no doubt you will struggle, as I do. This struggle is good as it shows the degree of difficulty in creating this mental construction and it also allows everyone to start the process because now they feel it's doable and not an uphill task. As you engage in this process, do it all the time and stay steady on this path, and be mindful that life will bring many distractions as opposites. Avoid the temptation to give in. This is the struggle that will take place; this is your training, your teaching moment, and your teacher. Don't they say when the student is ready, the teacher will appear? Choose the path your feelings have shown you, don't let the techno translation be lost as you move from feelings to thoughts, to words, and to deeds.

This is how my conversations began as I went through life. I collected it all together and began to write about each topic as I understood it, and over time, this became a routine. Whenever I had a question or wanted clarification on a subject matter, I used to create a thought and send it out. In time, the answer came back to me as a feeling. It was like an "Aha Aha!" moment. Many such moments came together to allow me to write this down and share it with all of you.

At times, I used to wonder if it was me doing the talking and me giving the answers. Then, I realized if I knew the answers, why would I ask the question to begin with? So this made me understand that a response was coming from a different source other than me. I knew my body and I knew my mind and so I concluded this must be my soul talking back to me. This made sense. I grew comfortable, and the conversation picked up speed and pace. Along I went, me asking for more or talking about what I knew, and then getting back something more insightful.

Here are some lines from our ancient books that add context and relate to my book:

John 10:30: *The Father and I are one.* – Meaning God as my soul is working with me and co-creating.

John 14:10: *Do you not believe that I am in the Father and the Father is in me? The words I say to you, I do not speak on my own: but the father, who dwells in me does his work.* – Meaning John and his soul are working together to do things. John made his connection and so can you.

John 14:11: *Believe me that I am in the father and the father is in me: but if you do not, then believe of the works themselves.* This your soul, John the apostle is talking about.

Luke 11:9: *So I say to you, ask, and it will be given to you; search, and you will find; knock, and the door will be opened.*—My book tells you this—Ask your soul and you will get what you ask.

Matthew 22:37: *Love your God with all your heart and with all your soul and with all your mind.*—There is your body, mind, and soul—the three aspects as mentioned 2,000 years ago.

The New Testament is full of such examples; many other religious books also carry similar messages, in different languages and in different ways. The prophets and the apostles spoke in parables, no one understood it at that time period in our history. We can now relate this clearly, words of wisdom spoken 2,000 years ago, never really understood fully. It's time to bring the meaning home now. My book can help you understand this ancient wisdom. It's time we shed the overemphasis we bring into religion and learn from the wisdom contained in it. Giving any religion more importance than the meaning it brings to us prevents us from understanding the true purpose. Understanding is everything; be it any religion, the message has always been the same, the delivery and the language has always been different. We confuse this and accept the difference, making it hard for us to know its true meaning. Once again, we see the physicality of the issue, not the metaphysicality of it. We miss the depth and own the surface.

So I ask all of you to start getting to know your soul and having that conversation. You may have other subjects, different themes and questions to ask, different topics than mine, so go ahead, and ask your soul. Our ancient scripture says, *"Ask and Ye shall get."* I asked and I got my reply, and so will you. Our ancestors communicated by a grunt and a sound; today we communicate in many different ways, face to face, phone to phone, e-mail to e-mail, chat lines to chat lines, and so on. It's time to get to know another way to communicate: Feelings to thoughts. While you have mastered the other ways, you will master this way too, but you need to start now. Relativity and physicality are two important tools we as humans are given to grow, develop, and evolve to become a higher being. Let's use this wisely and regularly and elevate ourselves to bring in metaphysicality to the two tools we now have as an additional tool. Relativity, physicality and now metaphysicality should become the new three tools to craft our life experiences.

So let me conclude by saying your journey in life is not complete until you make the first contact with your soul. This will uplift you to your next stage in evolution—The Hybrid Being—physical at some times and metaphysical at other times, with the power to move between these two stages at will. For this to happen, start a conversation today with your soul. The Universe is waiting for this to happen…
Are you ready, player one?